Contents

D0490427

Preface by Gordon Ramsay
Introduction by James Roose-Evans

Cook-a-Story
The Bleddfa Cook Book

Devised and edited by
James Roose-Evans

Preface by
Gordon Ramsay

Illustrations by
Quentin Blake CBE

Richard Briers

BLEDDFA BOOKS

BLEDDFA BOOKS
Published by The Bleddfa Trust

Copyright © 2005 The Bleddfa Trust.
Illustrations copyright © 2005, Quentin Blake.
All rights reserved.

The Bleddfa Trust extend their gratitude for all
the kind help, support and guidance from
Sally Carr, Hilary Laurie and the
David Cohen Family Trust.
Designed and typeset by Rafi Mohamed.
Printed and bound in China
by Everbest Printing Co Ltd.
This expanded and updated edition
published in July 2005.

THE **BLEDDFA CENTRE**
Bleddfa, Nr Knighton, Powys, LD7 1PA
t: 01547 550377   *f:* 01547 550370
e: enquiries@bleddfacentre.com
www.bleddfacentre.com

The Bleddfa Trust is a registered charity, no. 507635, and acknowledges
valuable support from the Welsh Arts Council, Powys County Council,
The Welsh Academi, Maryvale Farms and the Rufford Foundation.

Preface

Gordon Ramsay

Of the many cookbooks I have read, and they have been countless, here is one with a difference. James Roose-Evans has had the original idea of asking people to share their memories of a favourite, disastrous or hilarious meal. In concentrating on recipes, and the practicalities of cooking, we all too often forget those occasions on which we shared a memorable meal, whether celebrating a first love, a first baby, or a special gathering of friends - like the one that David Inshaw, the painter, describes when he and Peter Blake and other artists all used to share an annual working holiday in Cornwall. Perhaps the best compliment any chef can have is if, at the end of a meal, the guests begin to share memories, for good food should draw people together; it is a form of celebration, not simply a matter of calories. I think the greatest compliment I know of as a chef is when guests don't want to leave the table!

Introduction

James Roose-Evans

James is the founder and chairman of The Bleddfa Trust

Where, you may well ask, is Bleddfa, and how do you pronounce it? Strangely, for so tiny a hamlet, it has appeared on every map of the British Isles that I have seen. It is a scattering of farmsteads and cottages, with less than 100 inhabitants, in the least populated county in Great Britain - Radnorshire. Bleddfa possesses a 13th century church, the Hundred House Inn, its tiny sub-post office, open only on Thursday mornings - altogether an unlikely place to found any kind of centre. Yet over the past 30 years, which this book celebrates, people have been finding their way to the Bleddfa Centre for the Creative Spirit from as far afield as France, America and elsewhere, to take part in its various activities. The name itself in Welsh is thought to mean 'the place of the wolf' for wolves roamed wild here until Tudor times. Throughout the Middle Ages Bleddfa remained an isolated Lordship, the only Welsh land in the possession of a Herefordshire estate based at Richard's Castle near Ludlow. A castle was built in Bleddfa in the 12th century and a royal grant given to repair it in 1195, but it was not rebuilt after Llewelyn ap Gruffydd destroyed it in 1262. Only the mound on which it was built remains. In 1402 Owain Glyndwr's rebel army won a dramatic victory at Pilleth, on the eastern boundary of Bleddfa, against the English army of Sir Edmund Mortimer. Shortly before this, during the rising of 1401-2, parts of Bleddfa, including the church tower, are said to have been put to the torch by Glyndwr's men. And how is the word pronounced? The double 'dd' in Welsh is pronounced 'th' as in the word 'the', while the 'f' is

pronounced as 'v': thus it becomes 'Bleth-va'. In 1970
I bought the Old Rectory, and three years later the
then Rector informed me that the church, which
had a congregation of only four people, was on a
provisional list for closure. For a year I pondered
this, not really wanting to get involved, knowing full
well however that the only way to save a church
from closure was to re-activate it in some way. I
suggested that it be developed as a Centre for
Sacred Art, for exhibitions, concerts, retreats, study
days, on the principle that one has only to reach
out a hand to share and other hands will join that
first hand until a circle of friendship has been built
up. I am convinced that we have to rethink the
meaning of the word 'community' in connection
with rural areas. It should be apparent that, by and
large, the old unity of a village is already a thing of
the past. The increasing closure of village schools
and sub-post offices, the dwindling congregations
of churches and chapels, the drift of younger people
to towns and urbanised areas where there is a
greater chance of employment, plus the gradual
disappearance of the small farmer, have had the
effect in many places of debilitating rural areas. It
may be that future governments will arrest and
divert this movement but at present there is little
sign of this. If a village, especially a smaller one, is to
survive in this 21st century, it has to re-define the
meaning of that word 'community'. Each small
community will be forced to find its own solution
in pragmatic fashion. There is a Buddhist saying 'Look
at the ground on which your own feet stand'. One
starts with that which is at hand. In this instance I
set out to save the church. The late George Pace
RIBA, then the leading church architect in Britain,
and who had strong links with Wales, was
approached and generously gave his services for a
re-ordering of the building so that it could be used

for a variety of purposes. And then the long hard slog for funding began. By then we had discovered that the roof was held together simply by inertia, the wooden pegs holding each stone tile having long rotted. In the end the entire roof had to be re-battened, re-felted and re-tiled, one major beam replaced, two new sets of trusses installed, then pews taken up, the choir stall pit filled in, and much of the floor flagged, while the whole building was rewired. Since then, aided by a Lottery grant and funding from CADW, further restoration has been done, central heating installed, and new chairs purchased. Then in 1983 came the opportunity for what was known as the Bleddfa Trust, a registered charity, to acquire its own premises when sadly the village school closed due to lack of numbers. Aided by grants but also the contributions of many hundreds of people, the school was converted into a gallery, tearoom and shop, with a landscaped garden, and was formally opened on July 26th 1986 by the Marchioness of Anglesey. A few years later adjoining land plus some tumble-down barns were acquired where now stands the handsome Shaker-like Hall Barn, which comprises a large studio, reception area and small chapel, built around a central courtyard with a fountain. Today, as our current Director, Nicholas Colloff, has written: *In all the ebb and flow of fortune that the Bleddfa Centre has experienced in its thirty years' history this is perhaps the abiding vision: that the arts of the imagination, as Blake called them, are essential to a life, to communities that want to live to their full potential, to their full human, humane flourishing. It is an unapologetic vision - and one hard to live up to - providing opportunities for people to practise imagination, discover and enjoy its fruits in themselves and others, as a way towards discovering, revealing the Spirit in every aspect of our lives.*

James Roose-Evans

The Duchess of **Abercorn**

Barm Brack

At the time of writing the Duchess was doing therapeutic work with victims of violence in Northern Ireland.

The monks of medieval Ireland were for the most part a tolerant lot. They were constantly eager to expand their horizons with elements - especially secret elements - of the old Celtic religion. They were always on the look-out for new information. As a result they made a habit of recording their dreams and it was surprising how often they would learn something of value. And thus it was, on 1st April 1477, that two different monks - Brother Oswald in County Antrim and Brother Barnabas in County Clare - heard simultaneously of the mysterious ordinary delight called Barm Brack. According to their dreams, Barm Brack was a veritable food of the gods, which, once sampled by any mortal, made him or her attain extraordinary wisdom and perception. Unfortunately, however, when Brother Oswald in County Antrim woke from his dream, he could only remember the beginning part of it. In it he saw a regal lady in a crimson gown gently stirring a large black pot which had the word MAEV inscribed on the side of it. She was adding a pinch of nutmeg, a little more flour - a few more currants - but he could not, for the very life of him, remember the final ingredient.

Seemingly on the self same night in County Clare, Brother Barnabas had dreamt that he too had seen a majestic lady in a crimson gown stirring a big black pot which likewise had the word MAEV engraved on the side. She had been adding so many ingredients that he could only just remember the last two or three - currants, sultanas and cherries.

Both Brothers decided quite independently not to be outdone by such a trivial matter. In any case what could a mere woman, even though she may have had a queenly air about her, know about the preparation of this saintly food. They both decided to add an ingredient of their own so as to be able to produce this delicacy at the annual retreat.

Brother Oswald discovered a curious holly tree, growing in the monastery grounds, that had orange berries. As this was such a rarity he decided that the addition of a few berries would well make up for his missing ingredient. To his amazement his recipe turned out bright orange. Brother Barnabas, however, felt that a little green stag-moss would make up for his missing ingredient. To his amazement his recipe turned out bright green.

The day soon came for the two Brothers to meet at the annual retreat. It was not one of the happiest gatherings on record. Each Brother thought that he had discovered the true version of Barm Brack, and thus a mighty squabble ensued. Violence threatened to spoil the day until a wise abbot intervened and suggested that peace might be restored if the two recipes were combined. The result of this was the most delicious con-coction (which can still be sampled to this day). And naturally it was neither green nor orange - but instead a rich bog colour.

The two Brothers were incensed. They utterly failed to see how good the Barm Brack tasted. All they wanted to do was to claim full credit for it. So back to their respective monasteries they stormed in a terrible huff.

In the centuries that followed all records disappeared and the true origins of the dispute were forgotten. But it is not very hard to see that in the recipe for Barm Brack lies the original source of Ireland's troubles. The crucial ingredient was lost and will remain so, until the men of Ireland are prepared to listen to the voice of feminine wisdom in their dreams, or wherever else it may be found.

The recipe
1 lb warm flour
¼ teaspoon nutmeg
Pinch of salt
2oz butter
½oz yeast
2oz brown sugar
½pt milk
2 beaten eggs
8oz sultanas and 8oz currants
4oz mixed peel
3oz cherries quartered

Have all the ingredients at blood heat. Sieve the flour, nutmeg and salt together. Rub in the butter, cream the yeast with a little of the sugar. Add remaining sugar to the flour mixture. Warm milk; gently add the yeast and eggs. Reserve a little of the egg for glazing the bread. Beat liquid into dry ingredients until batter is stiff but elastic. Fold in the dry fruit and peel and turn into a buttered 8 inch cake tin. Cover with a cloth and put in in a warm place for one hour. Brush over with one tablespoon of sugar dissolved in a tablespoon or two of boiling water. Cook in oven for one hour, 190°C, or Gas Mark 5. Turn out and cool on a wire tray. Serve in slices with butter. When stale this is very nice toasted and buttered.

Myrtle Allen
RESTAURATEUR

Crêpe Suzette

Myrtle Allen runs Ballymaloe House in Co. Cork, Ireland

The most harassing problem in a restaurant kitchen is that of time. If a customer asks for something, he wants it immediately. Not in half an hour which would be convenient for the cook, who is already in the process of doing something else for several other people, who also want their orders immediately. One night at Ballymaloe some important guests sent an order to the kitchen for red currant sauce. I hadn't prepared any that night, but assured the waitress that I could make it in a minute from frozen fruit. I rushed to the freezer, a chest type, to get some. The freezer was almost empty, it is deep, and I am short and they were completely stuck to the floor. I literally dived in, legs in the air, but no matter how hard I pulled, I couldn't get out the bag. To break it meant scattering them everywhere. I imagined the guests furiously toying with their turkey, and impatiently demanding their sauce. I got redder in the face and my fingers more and more bruised. I wondered if they realised what it was like to be a restaurateur and not a customer. If they could see me, would they laugh?

There can be other hazards as once happened to me with a crêpe Suzette. Crêpe Suzette, the queen of the pancake family, is a party piece. It cannot be served to too many people at once, and so it goes onto our menu around Shrove Tuesday time, when oranges are at their best and restaurant numbers are down. I usually have to dress up and cook the crêpes myself for the customers at table. One evening I spruced myself up , put on a suitable little black dress, washed and set my hair so that it was all soft and fluffy, and arrived in the dining room ready for the performance. I proceeded to a table of about six people, all wanting crêpes. I followed the usual procedure of heating the pancakes on both sides in hot orange butter, folding them into fan shapes and arranging them around the edge of the pan, finally pouring in orange curaçao and brandy to flame them. Well, six people take quite a lot of pancakes, so I put in a good dash of the two liquors. They ignited with quite a bang - gave me a little shock in fact, but naturally I proceeded with the operation. After a minute, a waitress near me started to scream and a look of unusual consternation came over my customers. Then suddenly, a man jumped up from the table and enveloped my head in his serviette. I didn't know that I was calmly cooking with a halo of flames engulfing my lovely fluffy hair. 'Sit down,' they said, 'You must be suffering from shock.' In fact I was the only person in the dining room who was *not* suffering from shock: I hadn't noticed anything!

The recipe
(*Serves approximately 4*)
Pancake ingredients
55g (2oz or ½ cup) flour
Tablespoon oil
1 egg and 1 egg yolk
2 teaspoons orange curacao
150ml (¼ pt or two thirds cup) of milk
Put flour in bowl, make a well in the centre. Into this pour oil, egg, egg yolk and curaçao. Stir, gradually drawing in the flour from the sides as for ordinary pancakes. Add the milk slowly until it is a consistency of thin cream. Leave aside for 30 minutes.

Sauce ingredients
225g (½lb) large ripe oranges
85g (3oz or 6 tablespoons) softened butter
85g (2oz or 3/8) cup caster sugar
Grate rind of oranges very carefully so as not to penetrate the white. Add to butter and sugar; cream vigorously until smooth. To finish, assemble the following:
Frying pan (preferably copper for style)
Fondue stove
Matches
Fork and spoon
Orange butter
Pancakes
Caster sugar
Orange curaçao
Brandy
Hot pudding plates
Put the pan on a flame. Melt about 15g (½oz) orange butter in it. When bubbling, put the pancake in and heat throughout on both sides, turning. Fold it into a fan shape. Rest it against the side of the pan. Continue with the remaining pancakes. Sprinkle them with caster sugar. Pour over brandy and curaçao. Set alight, keeping your face away from the flames. Tilt the pan and spoon the juices over the pancakes until the flame subsides. Serve immediately on hot plates.

The Marquess of **Anglesey**

Eggs

The Marquess is a Patron of The Bleddfa Trust

It was Magdeburg, East Germany, 1945. The war was over; it had been won, but there were difficulties to be overcome with our Russian allies. My regiment, the Household Cavalry, had advanced eastwards to what was supposed to be the boundary between the two allies. We came up to a small river which marked the frontier. On the far side there were Russian soldiers. I shall never forget their unpleasing smell. We could scent it a long way off. Dressed in long overcoats and tall boots, they were very friendly as we shook hands with them. There was no hope of any conversation as the language barrier was insurmountable. We had been staring at each other for some time when a flock of geese started to walk towards us across the primitive footbridge. They were not halfway across before the Russians shooed them back again. The German farmer, whose farm was on both sides of the river, appeared and tried to reclaim his birds. We withdrew rather than take part in the tussle. The farmer lost his geese, and they soon lost their lives! We posted a few men to see that the Russians kept to their side, which they did. That evening all ranks not on duty assembled in an enormous barn at the request of the considerable number of Russian, Polish and other prisoners of war who had been employed by the farmer. There must have been twenty or thirty of them, plus the German labourers, and all of us. There was an unending supply of schnapps and other alcoholic drinks of which we partook liberally. Soon there was brought in a vast wooden bowl at least three feet in diameter, together with plates and large ladles. From it we helped ourselves to its contents: dozens and dozens of fried eggs! These were piled one on top of another, and further supplies were brought in as the coagulated mess was ladled out. Sliced bread too was provided in quantities. This is one of the most memorable meals in my life. Next day all the prisoners with whom we had shared it were loaded into Russian lorries to be taken home. They cheered and waved happily to us. Almost certainly these poor people, as we now know all too well, were at best put in labour camps but mostly executed. Prisoners of war were treated as deserters in Stalin's Russia. Talking of eggs, less than a year later I took a party to eat in a famous restaurant on the Thames, supposed, in spite of rationing, to supply good food. I had stomach trouble so I asked for a boiled egg. The waiter said, 'I'm sorry, sir, the egg chef is off tonight.' Those were the days!

Bronwen, Viscountess Astor

Smoked salmon pâté

I enjoy my salmon fishing. I fish on the Tweed, usually from a boat as the river is so wide. One day, many years ago, when I was still a novice, I hooked a very large salmon, around 18-20 pounds, and in the excitement of trying to land it, lost my footing and fell over in the boat. It was then I learnt the priorities of fishing: the gillie, ignoring me, grabbed the rod to save the fish! A fish as big as this gets smoked, and after it is eaten there are always bits left on the skin. It is these trimmings, some of them discoloured, that make this wonderful pâté.

The recipe
4oz smoked salmon trimmings
2oz Philadelphia cheese
2oz salted butter
1-2 tablespoons lemon juice
2 tablespoons sour cream
Sea salt and pepper
Chop and pound salmon trimmings in mortar or mixer. Beat in the cheese slowly. Add butter in small pieces, beat in sour cream, add lemon juice, salt and pepper. Pile into a small dish and chill. Serves 3-4 with toast.

Sir **Alan Ayckbourn**
PLAYWRIGHT

Christmas pudding

For many years I used to make the Christmas cake and the Christmas pudding. We now have a wonderful housekeeper who very discreetly took that chore over, but she continues to use the recipes I used. This is the one for the Christmas Pudding. It is fat free and it came from *The Times* when Shona Crawford Poole was its 'resident cook'. She described the pudding as having 'the full traditional flavour deceptively lightened'. I can endorse that.

The recipe (Serves 8 -10)
225g (8oz) stoned muscatels or other raisins
225g (8oz) currants
170g (6oz) fresh brown breadcrumbs
55g (2oz) blanched almonds or pecans, chopped
55g (2oz) glacé cherries, quartered.
55g (2oz) light muscovado sugar
2 tablespoons finely grated orange/tangerine zest
1 teaspoon ground cinnamon
1 teaspoon freshly grated nutmeg
¼ teaspoon ground cloves
3 large eggs
150ml (¼pt) port
6 tablespoons brandy
Put all the dry ingredients - the raisins, currants, breadcrumbs, nuts, cherries, sugar, zest and spices - into a large bowl and mix them thoroughly together. In another bowl whisk together the eggs, port and brandy. Pour the liquid over the dry ingredients and mix thoroughly. Butter a large pudding basin and put a circle of buttered greaseproof paper or baking parchment in the

bottom. This helps to stop the pudding sticking and breaking when you come to turn it out. Put the pudding mixture into the basin and cover it with buttered greaseproof paper and foil tied on tightly with string. It is important that no water gets into the pudding while it is cooking. Stand the pudding in a large saucepan and pour in boiling water to come about halfway up the sides of the basin. Bring the water back to the boil; reduce the heat to a gently bubbling simmer, cover the pan and steam the pudding for five hours. Check the water level from time to time, topping it up with boiling water as required.

Feed the pudding with a tablespoon or two more of brandy before covering it with fresh papers and storing it in a cool place. On Christmas Day steam the pudding for two hours.

This fatless Christmas pudding keeps every bit as well as more conventional mixtures. The quantities may be doubled or halved to make larger or smaller puddings without altering the cooking times, which are designed to maximise the flavour.

Richard Bawden
ARTIST AND ILLUSTRATOR

Crème caramel

Crème caramel is something I enjoy making. Everyone who tastes it thinks it supremely delicious. It is easy to make but there is a mystique about it. It is a favourite with my difficult 95-year-old mother-in-law. There was a memorable disaster, about fifty years ago, when Muriel Bose came to stay with my parents at Great Bardfield. She decided to make the family a Christmas treat and was left on her own in the kitchen to make her surprise. Which it was. The whole house hung with dense black smoke which lingered for days. My father Edward never let her forget it. So, here is how to make crème caramel without disaster.

The recipe
(For 4-5 portions, preparation time 8 minutes)
4 eggs
1 pt milk
2 tablespoons of white sugar, or natural off-white
1 teaspoon of vanilla, if you like.
Put sugar into a cast iron saucepan with 4 or 5 tablespoons of water, and stir with a wooden spoon whilst you get everything else ready, and stir from time to time. The mixture will become very hot, turning gradually yellow ochre, raw umber, burnt umber and, after a while, sepia, and finally deep black sepia. Put kettle on to boil. Mix eggs, milk and vanilla in bowl and whisk. Pour a little water into a Pyrex dish or heatproof bowl, ready for the caramelising sugar, and then pour away the surplus water. Open the window to let the black smoke depart. At this point the mixture should be almost sepia. Keep stirring and, if you

dare, add a few drops of hot water. Watch as it becomes very dark. Try some out on a white plate to see if it is the right colour. Don't panic. It might need another ten seconds. Now pour the bubbling morass into the Pyrex dish, making sure it covers the bottom. Let it settle. Pour the bowl of milk and egg mixture over the caramel. Stand in a large baking dish and pour in the hot water from the kettle around it. Put into the oven, which I should have mentioned should be pre-heated to 190°C Gas Mark 5. After half an hour open the oven door and pierce the créme caramel with a clean table knife. If it comes out clean the pudding is done. Put the pudding into the larder overnight. Go round the edges with a knife and turn out onto a decorative platter.

Lord **Beaumont** of Witley

Piperade

Disastrous meals seem to revolve round having guests who, for one reason or another, are important, and also round times when, for one reason or another, the hosts are employing servants. Failure meals for oneself may be sad but they are not disastrous.

I remember two such disasters. In the early sixties I formed, and for the most part entertained, a small dining-club of those of us who were trying to drag the Church of England into the modern world. Among the members, I recall, were Monica Furlong and Nicholas Mosley (both of whom incidentally had dreadful stammers and enjoyed arguing). We used to invite a guest to speak to us, and on this occasion the guest was Michael Ramsay, Archbishop of Canterbury, who spoke to us about what he saw as the dangerous growth of Evangelical Fundamentalism (and how right he was!). I think we must have gone slightly potty, for we had decided to serve a meal where all the courses were episcopally purple. We had a new cook and, overcome either by the culinary challenge or the eminence of the guest, halfway through the meal and before she got to the blackcurrant soufflé, she locked herself in her bedroom with a bottle of gin. Luckily she did not indulge in the classic, disastrous meal ploy of appearing in the dining room stark naked or wielding an offensive weapon.

That was reserved for a summer holiday at St Tropez where we had taken a delightful villa and had Clement and Jill Freud staying with us. The Mistral had been blowing, it was pouring with rain and we decided to have a lunch party to which, among others, Robin Day, his new wife, and Nigel Lawson were invited. We had just finished rather liberal pre-prandial drinks and were looking forward to lunch when all the lights went out and in burst the cook screaming, pursued by the *gardien* wielding a cleaver. Clement was magnificent and interposed himself between the two, explaining in fluent French that it would be inconsiderate to murder the cook at that moment as Monsieur Beaumont had some distinguished guests to lunch who were getting hungry. The *gardien* accepted that that was reasonable and allowed himself to be disarmed. The gendarmes, rung up, were not interested, because what can you expect when it is the Mistral. The *gardien* retired to sleep it off and we embarked on a splendid lunch starting with Piperade, a classic Basque dish made by scrambling buttered eggs with tomatoes and pimentos and served on fried ham on toast, of which I have been very fond ever since. Serve with large quantities of strong red wine.

Sister **Wendy Beckett**
HERMIT

Oeufs alpins

After many years in the teaching community (where, of course, I did no cooking) I was granted the privilege of coming to live in solitude here among the Carmelites at Quiddenham. I felt strongly that I did not want to spend my fairly limited energy in learning how to cook. Better to have cold food, and to try for the same food every day. My intention, to which I hold ever more firmly, is to keep my time for the intensity of prayer that alone justifies living in seclusion. But Delia Smith is a great friend to this monastery, and she insisted that cooking is such a simple matter that I should learn at least one hot dish, in case of emergencies. For me it was not at all simple, but I proudly present a dish I attempted twice, with success. I like its grandiloquent title, but since I have not tried again for twenty-five years, I am a little hazy about the details! However...

The recipe
Butter the sides and bottom of a small dish. Line with grated cheese. Break an egg, whip it up, and pour it in, layering it with the cheese. Cheese on top, as much as you have. Cook until cheese is crispy. Ten minutes? This is A VERY GOOD DINNER!

Tim Bentinck

ACTOR

Zabaglione

Archers listeners will know that David and Ruth are not qualified to write a cookery book - frozen pizzas and fish fingers are about all they can run to. I'm not much different - having married a wonderful cook, I am spoiled and pampered, but occasionally wheeled out to perform my specialities: an artistic and ad-libbed Spaghetti Bolognese, or a rare fillet steak with asparagus and new potatoes. I'm also a dab hand at mackerel, since you hardly need to do anything to them except add a dab of butter and wrap them in aluminium foil.

I have left zabaglione out of my repertoire after a disaster at drama school. I had been appointed pudding-meister for a large dinner at our flat for a group of friends that, at the time, sounded perfectly normal, but written down now sounds like massive name-dropping. Such was the quality of teaching we got at the Bristol Old Vic School, most of these names are now much more familiar: Daniel Day-Lewis, Amanda Redman, Greta Scacchi, Jenny Seagrove, Miranda Richardson, Nicholas Farrell and David Heap. My mistake was to make the zabagliones in their wine glasses the night before and leave them in the fridge, even though that's what the recipe told me to do. I sampled one and it was delicious, light, airy, alcoholic and perfect. The next day they had all gone totally flat. Ms Seagrove came round to help me revive them but, despite strenuous whipping and large portions of gelatine, they remained resolutely un-frothy, flat and lifeless. Minutes before the meal was due to start, I shot out in the car and bought two enormous ready-made cheesecakes from 'Good Food'. I've never made, or even eaten zabaglione since. But here is the recipe!

The recipe
Ingredients
4 large egg yolks
1/3 cup of sugar
1/3 cup of dark rum
1/3 cup dry Marsala wine
1 cup heavy cream, beaten to a medium-thick consistency.

Directions
In a large deep bowl beat eggs and sugar until thick and pale yellow. Set on top of a smaller saucepan, over simmering water. Slowly add the rum and Marsala and beat well with a whisk or electric mixer until fluffy, doubled in size and hot. Set over iced water and stir till cool. Gently fold in cream. Cover and refrigerate several hours or overnight.

Beshlie
ROMANY ARTIST

Romany meals

January 3rd 1986   We are in a field owned by Travellers, near Bicester. At 3*am* on Christmas Eve we had to get up and dress as flood waters were rising all round us! The worry was for the outside dogs in their kennels, and the electric flex plus sockets at ground level as, of course, all the traveller-style trailer homes are connected to mains. After Christmas, with the decorations still up, we had to pack our Crown Derby, Worcester and other plate, and move to slightly higher ground, but it is very exposed, with lots of high winds that frequently change from North East to South West, so we have to keep changing the direction of the chimney cowl otherwise the room fills with fumes! I hope your life is rather more placid. I am sending you two recipes.

Charcoal burner's victuals

An old man, whose father was the Bodger, had once been a charcoal burner. He told me of this meal which he cooked on a slow heat of charcoal. I have alterered several contents in order to adjust to today's tastes, using butter instead of mangols[†], rice instead of potatoes, and have left out altogether the pheasant's eggs, duck, moorhen or hen, but I have broken two eggs on the top shortly before serving. The old man, who went by the name of Black Jack, long after he had turned to carpentry, could imitate many hedgerow birdcalls, and in his youth was skilled at bird catching, using call-birds and nets, making his own cages from white willow. Bodger, a maker of chair legs, worked in the woods, cutting the

† *(A form of beet)*

wood and turning the legs which he then sold to the chairmaker.

The recipe
Place 2oz butter in shallowish pan which has a lid. Slice in a large onion. Put lid on. Peel 2 thick carrots; cut downwards into four, and chop across each section. Add this to the pan with some marjoram. Peel a large parsnip and cut downwards into eight pieces, and chop each section into one-inch pieces. Add to the pan and put in a cupful of water. Replace lid. Cook on low heat. Prepare one dozen sprouts and cut into thin slices, place in a dish with 1oz of mixed fruit (dried as for cakes). Add two cupfuls of cooked rice to the vegetables, stir and place on top of the sprouts and mixed fruit. Replace lid. The rice will absorb the liquid. This should only take about 5 minutes. Serve with a large spoonful of blackcurrant jelly in centre of individual bowls. Remember, it is important to use victuals in given order. Other dried herbs can be used instead of marjoram. Place in the pan with the onion before the liquid. The butter retains the flavour. We eat this meal with Winter Cress, known also as Yellow Rocket (*Barbarea vulgaris*) obtainable all winter. Transfer a plant of it to your garden in the autumn.

Flowers-of-Rye
A lady, known to my Grandfather, to whom I was sent as a child with a weekly basket of 'goodies', as she was too large to emerge from her door! showed me how to cook these pancakes, and she also introduced me to the taste of sweet-apple, sugared pancake, marmalade and cream - so much nicer than the conventional lemon. I often mix maize flour in with the rye for taste, and for the golden colour.

The recipe

Place in a small bowl enough rye flour to make two pancakes. Break in one large egg, mix well with a fork, and when all flour is involved, add enough milk to make it easy to pour, but not runny. Leave to stand while peeling (not coring) a sweet apple. Hold top and bottom by middle finger and thumb, and slice off equal sized slices. The core will be left in the hand! Heat a goodly quantity of vegetable oil and butter in a shallow pan. When it is hot, but not smoking, pour in the batter, shake pan, and while on the heat, arrange apple slices quickly in a ring like flower petals. The outer edge of the batter should form 'points'. Keep the heat low, lift corner to see if cooked, then turn over. Cook apple side for same length of time. Place a plate onto pan and turn out onto plate. Serve with nuts and raisins or two spoonfuls of marmalade and cottage cheese or cream. Also nice with candied fennel stems.

Sir **Peter Blake**
ARTISTS

Trompe l'eel

The menu reproduced on the right is the most extraordinary meal I have ever had. It was given to celebrate the opening of the Otsuka Museum of Art in Naruto, Japan. The museum recreates pretty much every work of art ever made - in enamel! You enter the museum on a very long escalator, rather like the one in *A Matter of Life and Death*, and when you step off it you are facing a full-sized Sistine chapel flanked by two other chapels. The Gala dinner took place beneath Michaelangelo's mural - in enamel! Next day at the private view I remember there were two enormous tins of caviar, which never seemed to get any lower, and you could eat baby eels which, having been frozen, came back to life with the warmth of your throat. Unfortunately I didn't try them!

MENU

Japanese Appetizer

Stuffed Sudachi Octopus with Plum Paste
Grilled Bamboo Shoot with Sea Urchin
Braised Small Abalone
Naruto Renkon Chips
Boiled Broad Beans

Beluga Caviar on Ice served with Condiments

Saut'eed Foi Gras with Truffle Flavor

Traditional Ise Lobster Consomme'

Naruto Sea Bream Harmonic with Awaji Sea Urchin

Plum Wine Sherbet

Stewed Selected Cheek of Awa Beef
in Classic Bordeaux style

Assorted Cheese
and Champagne with Apple

Blanc-Manger decorated
with Gold Powder

Petits Fours

Coffee
Blue Mountain

Rabbi **Lionel Blue**

A fishy tale

A sad man goes into a restaurant during Chanukah, the December *Feast of Lights Festival*. With tears in his eyes he tells the waiter, 'I am now like an orphan. Bring me some fish balls just like the ones my poor dear mother used to make.' As the waiter turns to go, he clutches the waiter's arm. 'And also give me a kind word,' he asks piteously. Some minutes later the waiter returns. Without comment he puts a plate of fish balls before the diner, and then turns to go. Again the man clutches him. 'And what about my kind word?' he begs. The waiter considers and then bends down and whispers in the man's ear, 'If I were you, I wouldn't touch our fish.'

Michael Bond

AUTHOR AND CREATOR OF PADDINGTON BEAR

Artichokes

When it comes to food, French enterprise knows no bounds. If it grows at the side of the road or moves on the ocean bed, it is only a matter of time before it lands on someone's plate. Or so it seemed in 1950 when my then wife, Brenda, and I encountered our first artichoke. We were honeymooning in St.Briac, a few kilometres round the coast from Dinard, and having been brought up in war-time Britain, we had no idea what to do with it. Since it arrived without any instructions, we set to work on the leaves, hoping things might get better as we went along. To say we found them hard going is an understatement, but as the Hotel du Centre enjoyed a star in the Michelin guide and I was already a confirmed Francophile, I maintained the chef must know what he was doing and that artichokes were an acquired taste. Being first for dinner, we acted as trendsetters, and as the other guests, all English and equally inexperienced, arrived downstairs to join us, they followed suit. The dining room went very quiet until eventually the chef popped his head round the door to see why everyone was taking so long. His white hat nearly fell off. Clearly he couldn't count on having an early night.

There was worse to come. Having decided to spend what was left of our meagre travel allowance on a final gastronomic blow-out, we had placed an advance order for *Homard à l'americaine* followed by *Soufflé au Grand Marnier*; both dishes that were listed in the Michelin as the chef's specialities. They were delicious, far beyond anything we had experienced before. First of all the fresh lobster arrived, swimming in butter and cognac; then came the omelette, resplendent on a vast silver platter, foaming at the mouth and reeking of Grand Marnier. Having finished their set menu, the other guests silently gathered round to watch us at work, but by then we were past caring. Afterwards we encountered many of them shuffling penguin-like round the village, barely able to move, let alone bend down. Nobody spoke to us. It was several years before we tackled another artichoke and by then we knew the ropes. Having savoured the tips and salivated over the heart, I gaily emptied the bowl of discarded leaves into our newly acquired waste disposal unit. After a couple of half-hearted revolutions it seized up. I couldn't complain. From past experience, I knew exactly how it felt!

Artichoke: *A member of the thistle family... The eater must be equipped with front teeth and patience... The British do not eat artichokes much.*

~ THE OXFORD COMPANION TO FOOD

Lord **Melvyn Bragg**
BROADCASTER AND WRITER

Meanz tested

Without trying to be modest, I'm most certainly in the world's top ten indifferent / bad cooks. I'm just not a foodie and I like what I like and I have it again and again. The restaurants I go to don't even ask anymore - they just put it on the table! My wife tries to sneak in a few new things every now and again, but I'm usually sufficiently alert to spot them. If you really want me to join in properly, the best I can give you (true) is a full tin of Heinz Baked Beans on brown toast, lightly buttered, with some cooked tomatoes (the real test is to get them all hot at the same time), followed by dark chocolate and a glass or two of red wine. The latter is the only thing I added on since I learnt it in the 2nd Troop of the Wigton Boy Scouts in the early 1950s.

Giles Brandreth
WRITER AND PERFORMER

Spanish Pap

Recently I have been living in a time warp. (Those who know me will now be gasping, *'Recently?!'*) I mean, in fact, that I have been living in a proper time warp, a culinary time warp. My wife, Michele, has been compiling a book of historical recipes and decided that in the year 2004 we should eat, exclusively, food as it would have been eaten in 1604! The eel pie was a struggle and I gagged on the pike pudding, but I simply adored a dessert called Spanish Pap. Don't be put off by the name; it's delicious. It is basically a custard made from cream and egg yolks, often thickened with a little rice flour and flavoured with orange flower water. The use of these flower waters, rose water and orange flower water in particular, became extremely popular at this time. Almond tart combines this popular flavour with another, almonds, which were being properly cultivated in England at this (time?) period.

The recipe (Serves 6)
225g (8oz) flour weight, puff pastry
100g (4oz) unsalted butter
125ml (¼ pint) single cream
125ml (¼ pint) double cream
100g (4oz) ground almonds
4 tablespoons orange flour water
½ tablespoon caster sugar
1 teaspoon ground nutmeg
Pinch salt
3 egg yolks
Line a 20cm (8inch) flan tin with the pastry. Melt the butter in the cream gently in the top of a

double boiler. Add the almonds, orange flower water, sugar, nutmeg and salt. Heat a little longer until the mixture thickens. Leave to cool. Beat the egg yolks together and beat them into the cooled almond cream. Pour into the prepared flan case and bake at 180°C Gas Mark 4, until the filling sets (about 45 minutes). Sprinkle with caster sugar and serve, preferably while still warm.

Richard Briers
ACTOR

The Good Life

Although I have been won over by certain aspects of international good living - French wines, Indian curries - in my heart of hearts I think of the Good Life as essentially an enjoyment of all that is best in British food and drink. The way to a man's heart is through his stomach and home is where the heart is, to coin a cliché or two. Some years ago, during a Shakespearian world tour organised by the one and only Kenneth Branagh, we visited Tokyo, where, for me, it was difficult to find any decent food. I am the first to admit that I am not 'good at abroad' and only Ken could have got me this far from Charing Cross Road. Annie is far more adventurous gastronomically than I am, and sampled raw fish with relish. Personally, I just cannot understand why the Japanese don't bung all those excellent ingredients into a frying pan, and then we could all have a good meal. Why does raw fish require the services of a chef at all! After a couple of days of virtual self-starvation one of my fellow actors informed me that there was a restaurant that served fried dishes. I was there like a shot. The food came, and there before me were several golden oblong shapes in thick batter. I cut the top off the first delicious-looking offering and out shot a claw - I didn't wait to find out what kind. After that I stuck to cheese sandwiches and Japan's finest saki.

Marina Cantacuzino
JOURNALIST

Verza de Cluj *(Cabbage of Cluz)*

I remember this recipe from my childhood, cooked by my grandmother when we visited her in her ramshackle cottage during the cold winter months. My grandmother, who came to live in England during the Second World War as a Rumanian refugee, told us the dish came from Transylvania and was part of the Rumanian peasant's staple diet. Arriving in England penniless and leaving behind a life of wealth and privilege, she was used to food being served by a staff of cooks and kitchen maids. For the first time in her life she had to think about planning and preparing meals. A thoughtful relative smuggled her out a pocket-size Rumanian recipe book from which she learned the rudiments of cookery. By the time we were around she had become a brilliant cook. Varza de Kluj was always everyone's favourite.

The recipe
1 small cabbage
5oz sauerkraut
1lb lean minced meat
6oz tomato purée
1 stock cube dissolved in a mug of hot water
1 medium onion
½oz butter
2 medium tomatoes
4oz sour cream
Salt and pepper
½ teaspoon of oregano
½ teaspoon of basil
Slice the cabbage and boil in salted boiling water until cooked. Mix with sauerkraut and leave to

one side. Chop onions finely and simmer in butter. Mix in tomato purée, stock cube dissolved in water, and seasoning. Take off the heat and mix with the meat. Grease a medium-size oven dish and place a layer of cabbage at the bottom followed by a layer of meat. Repeat twice, finishing with a layer of meat. Slice the tomatoes and place over the top. Bake in a pre-heated oven at 180°C Gas Mark 4, for approximately one hour. Serve with sour cream.

Lord **Alex Carlile** of Berriew QC

Beetroot soup *(Barszcz)*

This is the easiest soup in the world to make. My Mother was born in Vienna in 1914, to Polish Jewish parents. She was brought up comfortably in the historic city of Lwow, now in Ukraine but then in Poland. Everything fell part in 1941, when the collapse of the Hitler/Stalin Pact led to Lwow becoming part of the war. From then until 1945 she was on the run or in hiding, and fought in the Warsaw uprising of 1944 so tellingly depicted in 'The Pianist'. By the end of the war she had little in the way of possessions; her most cherished personal item was an eiderdown, which she had managed to carry throughout. Her parents were still alive, but she had lost her husband, brother and other close relatives to persecution and armed struggle.

When she came to Britain in 1945, and shortly afterwards married my father, she brought little in the way of possessions. However, she retained a remarkable talent for cooking, and a fund of Polish recipes, which even at nearly 90 years old she can prepare to near perfection. One is this traditional recipe for beetroot soup. It has become part of Christmas in our family: we always start our Christmas dinner with this simple and delicious dish. Its bright colour is in itself part of the decorated table. The quantities are very approximate. This is not accidental. The creative peasant Polish mother can vary it according to available ingredients.

The recipe
2 pints ham or bacon stock
4 uncooked beetroot
Juice of ½ squeezed lemon
Chopped parsley
Crushed clove of garlic
Cream (can be soured cream)
Grate the beetroot; this can be done very fast with a food processor. Add to stock and cook for 5 - 7 minutes. Add crushed garlic and lemon juice to taste. Serve with a sprinkle of parsley and a swirl of cream. The soup should remain bright red. Do not overcook.

John Cleese
ACTOR AND WRITER

Cornflakes

This is an excellent dish and here is the story behind it. I once had to arrange a rather distinguished dinner party. However, the guests were not only eminent, but pre-eminent in their fields, and also came from a wide variety of backgrounds. They included: the Duke of Kent, Little and Large, Brian Clough, Boy George, Yoko Ono, Rev Ian Paisley and Buzz Aldrin. I anticipated conversation might be a little sticky to start with, so I felt that the best way to break the ice was with a traditional Creole dish that I had first encountered in Dalmatia - the natives call it 'Cornflakes'.

The recipe
Buy a packet of cornflakes.
Open the cardboard box.
Open the sort of plastic packet inside the box.
Pour the contents (sort of yellowy brownish bits of things) onto a plate.
Buy a bottle of milk.
Take the top off the thin end of the bottle.
Invert the bottle gently over the Cornflakes making sure that the milk does not go over the edge of the plate.

It's very simple to make and absolutely delicious. An alternative is to use Coca-Cola instead of milk. Add basil as required.

Stephanie Cole
ACTOR

Hot chocolate

As a child brought up by the sea in a little village in Devon, one of my favourite memories is of Sunday mornings and the smell of frying bacon. Down I would come to the kitchen, drawn irresistibly towards the old Aga, and in the bacon fat would be laver bread (seaweed) being fried. Oh, bliss! Chocolate was another delight and, being something of a chocoholic, here is a quick way to get a fix:

1oz unsalted butter
I tablespoon Golden Syrup
I tablespoon organic dark chocolate powder
Heat and mix, and hey presto! the best hot chocolate there is.

Peter Conradi
AUTHOR

Toad in the whole

'Food' the narrator (Charles Arrowby) of Iris Murdoch's Booker-prize-winning novel *The Sea, The Sea* (1978) asserts, 'is the one subject about which writers never lie'. Indeed, one feature that attracted attention was Charles's comically disgusting and inventive recipes, some, as I recall, involving bloater paste and ketchup. When Anthony Storr protested about some of these improbable combinations to Dame Iris at a College dinner, she riposted, sounding surprised, 'But this is what John and I *eat all the time*'. 'Wind-in-the Willows food', someone joked about this caisine. John Bayley - whose trousers bore such exciting food-stains that a horse in Ireland once attempted to take a bite out of them - did the cooking for dinner-parties, reheating College food. Once he attempted an ambitious *'sauce verte'* for the Anthony Powells, A.N. Wilson and Katharine Duncan-Jones, recalled fondly years later as tongue-in-green-slime. A much-heralded 'surprise-pudding of Iris's', to general astonishment and after quite a long build-up, consisted in each guest being awarded, from off a huge tray, a single Mr Kipling cake.

Christopher Cook
BROADCASTER

Herb and Parmesan scones

I've always loved picnics. Not your English countryside or seaside picnics with those kamikaze midges dive-bombing plump flesh, or the sand dunes that get into the sandwiches. No, thank you. What I like are urban picnics as part of a visit to the opera, or an art gallery or the concert hall. Something to nibble on between Rubens and Rembrandt or to keep your strength up during a long Wagnerian interval. And carefully planned too, so as to match the pictures or the music, although my *Oeufs en geleé Isolde* cannot really be counted as a triumph and I've never yet managed a proper *Fête champêtre* at the Wallace Collection in London amidst the mouth-watering Watteaus and those succulent Bouchers!

One late-September Sunday my carefully-laid picnic plans went terribly awry. I had quite forgotten that I had promised to accompany an American friend to William Morris's house in Walthamstow. I'd provide the food and he'd feed us the art history. As dawn broke on the appointed day even Mother Hubbard would have despaired at the contents of my store cupboard and freezer, just the last of the summer's tomato soup and a heel of Parmesan. But no bread. Now only a truly desperate man buys bread on a Sunday when all that remains on shop shelves is Saturday's leftovers or baked blancmange coffined in plastic after a ritual murder with chemicals to keep it 'fresh'. However, good soup cries out for good bread. Not on this occasion. Inspiration struck; the kitchen muse took pity on me. Why not scones? Savoury scones with Parmesan. And

45

better still, scones flavoured with the last of the summer herbs from the window box. If necessity is the mother of invention, then in the kitchen improvisation is her fairy godmother! The scones were delicious, matching the soup and William Morris's weaving admirably. So good, that now I even make them when there's no soup and no picnic in view either.

The recipe
(Makes about 10 decent-sized scones)
Ingredients
225g plain flour
2 teaspoons baking powder
¼ teaspoon salt
50g butter
55g fresh Parmesan finely grated
1 tablespoon chopped parsley
2 teaspoons chopped thyme or marjoram or sage
¼ freshly ground pepper
Approx 150ml milk
Method
1. Heat the oven to 220°C Gas Mark 7
2. Sift together the flour, baking powder and salt
3. Swiftly rub in the butter until mixture resembles bread crumbs
4. With a knife stir in the cheese, the herbs and ground pepper
5. Add 150ml milk and mix to firm dough
6. Roll out on floured board to a thickness of about 1½cm
7. Cut out 5cm rounds and put on a greased and floured baking tray
8. Brush the tops with milk and bake for about 12-15minuts
9. The tops should be gently golden
10. Leave to cool on a wire rack

Ian Curteis and **Joanna Trollope**
AUTHORS

Alvin's chocolate cake

Living as we did in the valley of a trout stream, we were blessed not only with domestic processions of duck and moorhen past the windows, but also with creaking fly-pasts of swans, winging westward from Buscot Park. They were mutes, elegant and unamiable, and occasionally alighting to graze picturesquely in the water meadows beyond the stream. In the snowy winter of 1985, a particular lone swan, a powerful old cob, heaved himself out of the river onto our bank and began a laborious flap-footed journey up the lawn to the house. It was a considerable undertaking, involving two flights of stone steps and a gravel path, but he made it right to the kitchen window and took up his stand there, honking imperiously for food. From behind the safety of glass, we christened him Alvin. The local swan rescue service told us to feed our guest on brown bread, green salad stuff and cracked wheat. He thought little of the bread, and nothing at all of the watercress and the wheat, which he stood on. Nevertheless, he came every day, persistent and picky, until he hit by chance upon a family birthday. There was a cake, a particularly good cake, made with ground almonds rather than flour, filled with black cherry jam and darkly chocolatey. A slice was cut and laid before Alvin. One bite, and he was hooked, an instant addict of the cocoa bean like everyone else since Montezuma. He ate every last crumb and then, replete and triumphant, made his leisured way back to the river, his orange beak smeared with chocolate and, reposing on his gleaming bosom like a jewel, a single cherry from the jam.

The recipe
5oz dark chocolate
4oz dark brown sugar
2oz ground almonds
3 big eggs, separated
6 fluid oz whipping cream
6 tablespoons water
4oz soft margerine
2oz white bread with the crusts cut off
Black cherry jam
Butter a 7-8 inch cake tin and line it with buttered grease-proof paper. Melt 4oz of the chocolate in the water and allow to cool a little. Beat the brown sugar and the soft margerine together until they are light and fluffy, then beat in the egg yolks, the almonds and the chocolate. Whizz the bread in a food processor until it becomes crumbs, and stir them in too. Heat the oven to 190°C Gas Mark 5. Whisk the egg whites until they are stiff, and fold them carefully into the chocolate mixture with a metal spoon. Pour the mixture into the cake tin and bake for 40-50 minutes. It is ready when the centre bounces back after a light touch. Cool it in the tin. When it is cold, slice it in half and spread the middle thickly with black cherry jam. Whip the cream and spread that over the whole cake, using the last ounce of chocolate to grate over the top. Then look for a swan to offer it to.

Roald Dahl
AUTHOR

Oxtail stew

Despite the fact that I am a very ordinary cook indeed, my oxtail stew, every time I make it, is greeted with exclamations of relish and sometimes even loud applause. By some fluke rather than by any real skill, it always seems to come out right. So, for what it is worth, I shall tell you as best I can how to make it.

1. Always buy more than you think you'll need. Oxtail is so delicious that most people are inclined to ask for second and even third helpings. I allow one tail for every three guests, and if I'm feeding nine or ten, I will always buy four. Ask the butcher to chop them up. Most good butchers keep oxtail in stock frozen rather than fresh, but it makes no difference.

2. Always trim off the fat and gristle.

3. I don't bother to brown them in fat before boiling. I've come to the conclusion it makes little difference. Simply bung all the oxtail pieces into a large saucepan, cover them with water and get the whole thing boiling gently. Shove in a lot of beef stock cubes, six at least.

4. The main secret of this dish is to make absolutely sure that the meat is very well cooked. It should be almost falling off the bone when served. This will require roughly four hours boiling. Towards the end, keep taking out a piece and testing it.

5. While the tails are cooking, boil some carrots and then purée them in the blender or food processor. This will ultimately be the only thickener you use for the liquid. No flour.

6. About fifteen minutes from the end, throw in plenty of medium-sized onions.

7. Examine your bottles of dried herbs and make an instinctive selection, choosing the ones you particularly like. Perhaps rosemary, basil and mixed herbs. Use liberally.

8. Three minutes from the end add whatever frozen vegetables you have. I favour broad beans, sweet corn and peas. The quantity of each is a matter for your own judgement.

9. Lastly, thicken the liquid with your purée of carrots.

You now have a lovely, rich, pungent oxtail stew. Serve in soup plates with plenty of hot French bread. Have a large dish on the table into which people can throw their used bones.

As you can see, this oxtail stew recipe is about as vague and imprecise as a recipe could be. But it is fun to cook like that, using your own judgement all the time, throwing in a bit of this and a bit of that, tasting it constantly and never consulting the cookbook.

Dame **Judi Dench**
ACTRESS

Barbados cream

This is very quick, easy and delicious. The memory I have is of making it for supper when Eric and Joan Morecombe came. They also brought a beautiful bottle of champagne, which I put in the fridge. Just before dinner, I went to get something out of the fridge and the champagne bottle fell out and smashed on the floor. Joan and Eric asked about the noise and I passed it off as something else. At the end of dinner, after eating the Barbados cream, Eric said, 'Now, let me guess what smashed on the floor.....the pudding!'

The recipe
2 small cartons plain yoghurt
1 small carton double cream
Whip the cream and mix together with the yoghurt until smooth. Divide into small bowls or ramekins and top with a thick layer of soft brown sugar. Refrigerate for at least two hours before serving.

Christopher Fry
PLAYWRIGHT

The Bedfordshire Clanger

It is strange how some of the simple cooking eaten in childhood stays in the mind, and the magnificent dishes of later years disappear from memory. I remember vividly the rissoles my mother used to cook - dark with meat, crisp on the outside, and green with parsley, though what her recipe was, if she had one, I don't know. The famous local thing to eat (I was brought up in Bedford) for the workers in the field, or countryside explorers on their bicycles, was the Bedfordshire Clanger. It had the advantage over the Cornish pasty in being two courses in one, the meat and the pudding.

The recipe
To make the pastry use 4oz of plain flour, I teaspoon of baking powder, ½ teaspoon of salt, 2oz of beef suet, and water to mix. To make the filling: 5oz of meat cut into small pieces (stewing beef or bacon is best); diced potatoes and chopped onion in small amounts; seasoning to taste; stock or gravy or water; approximately 2 dessertspoons of jam (plum or apricot are good, important to choose a firm kind). Make pastry and shape it into an oblong, keeping a piece of the pastry to make a bridge between the two courses. Spread the meat potatoes and onions on the larger section, season to taste and moisten with a little gravy or stock. Spread jam on the other section (about a third of the whole) Roll up with care, seal edges with water, then lightly flour the Clanger, wrap it in buttered or greaseproof paper, and a pudding cloth, and secure. Put it in boiling water and simmer for approximately two hours. Best eaten under a hawthorn bush in May.

Christopher Good
ACTOR

Spaghetti Bolognese

This was my choice for a house-warming lunch-party for twenty friends in my new flat close to Kilburn High Road (North London) in the early '70s, the day after I moved in. I prepared everything on a tiny Baby Belling cooker (which I still use after thirty years). The guests arrived and, after being fortified with plentiful wine, we sat down to a starter of chicken liver pâté with brandy. I went back into the kitchen to cook the spaghetti. This was accomplished. I heaped the steaming mound onto a magnificent 'Asiatic Pheasant' serving dish and poured the generous sauce on top. As I carried the weighty dish to the door I slipped on some olive oil on the floor (I always use it lavishly!) Somehow, I managed to save the dish but the entire mountain of spaghetti - plus sauce - ended up on a less-than-clean floor. Without a second's hesitation I scooped up the food with my bare hands (it was VERY hot!) and flung it back on the dish, lavishly garnished it with even more parsley, washed my scalded hands and dramatically entered the dining room. Nobody had the slightest idea what had just occurred. Generous seconds were relished by all.

Spaghetti Bolognese
(Sauce to be prepared at least one day in advance.)
1 large onion, chopped
1 shallott, chopped
3 cloves of fresh garlic, crushed and chopped
1 tin chopped tomatoes
1lb ripe tomatoes, skinned and de-seeded
1lb best minced beef

10 or more black olives, pitted and chopped
Good red wine
Olive oil
Mixed fresh herbs, chopped
Fresh parsley, chopped
Salt and freshly ground black pepper
Sauté chopped onion in olive oil; add fresh tomatoes; cook gently for 5 minutes and remove from heat. In a separate pan, gently glaze the shallot and garlic in olive oil. Add the mince, stirring constantly to prevent sticking. When this has browned, add the onion and tomato mixture, stirring the while. Add the tin of chopped tomatoes with red wine, herbs and salt and pepper to taste. Combine well and simmer, very gently, for 30 minutes. Leave until cold and place in fridge until required. On the day, put sauce in to a casserole and heat thoroughly in a medium oven for about 30 minutes. To a pan of boiling and salted water add enough spaghetti for six and cook *al dente* (approximately 12 minutes). Serve with freshly chopped parsley.

Robin Hanbury-Tenison
EXPLORER

Paella

After Louella and I were married, we went on a series of long distance rides around the world: bringing Camargue horses back to Cornwall from the south of France; along the Great Wall of China; through New Zealand; on the Pilgrimage to Santiago de Compostella and, finally, driving big, black cattle across Spain on the legendary *transhumancia*. For two blistering weeks we worked as *vaqueros*, cowboys, driving 300 beautiful but obdurate long-horned cows from Extremadura to Avila, through cork forests, across dusty plains and, following an ancient Roman Road, over the Sierra de Credos. From six in the morning to eleven at night, we cantered ftom side to side of the herd, shouting *'anda'* and *'vaca'* until we were hoarse, and then slept exhausted on the ground wrapped in our blankets. Louella was the first woman to do this and by the end our four companions, traditional vaqueros, who had not met a blonde before, were all in love with her. The last day was her fortieth birthday and they prepared a gigantic *paella* to celebrate both that and our safe arrival.

Paella is the traditional Spanish rice dish, and its name comes from the flat round pan with handles in which it is cooked and served. That day ours was well over a meter across - a double or treble serving - but usually they are smaller About 3*lbs* of assorted fish and shellfish such as crawfish, prawns, mussels, cockles and squid are cleaned and fried with garlic in oil. 2 sliced lemons and ½*lb* of tomato and a green pepper are added, and sometimes breast of chicken and loin of pork as well. Lastly 1 *lb* of rice is stirred in and left to absorb the oil before a quart of boiling chicken stock is poured on, followed by sliced *chorizo*, some bay leaves and cloves and, to give the whole dish its glorious yellow colour, a ½ teaspoon of saffron. The whole is covered and simmered for about 30 minutes.

Elizabeth and **Charles Handy**
PHOTOGRAPHER   MANAGEMENT WRITER

Roast peppers with anchovies

I love vegetables with colours - they remind me of sunshine and especially sitting on our terrace in Italy. I try to transfer that feeling to England. The following recipe is one that tastes delicious in England, but even more delicious in Italy. Charles and I share the cooking between us. Charles finds cooking a great antidote to the pains of writing books - you get instant feedback when you cook a meal, he says, instead of having to wait a year for the book to come out, and people are still amazed that he, a mere male, can do these things! When he uses this recipe he does a slight variation on mine. I have started to do 'still life' photographic portraits of people. This dish is so beautiful and conjures up so many memories that I think I would like to include this recipe if I had to do a still life of myself. Recently I experimented with serving it differently too. I used to take the skins off the peppers which was rather time-consuming and difficult, and usually ended up with me over-doing the grilling so they came out black. (I used to grill the peppers until the skins were bubbly - turning them over on each side and so usually burning my fingers - then put the peppers in a couple of plastic bags and after half an hour the skins were meant to peel off easily.) I have stopped doing all that now!

The recipe
Allow one red and one yellow pepper for every two persons. Slice the peppers in half, taking care to cut out the core and seeds so that each half pepper has a bit of a lip to it - to hold the other

ingredients. Salt and pepper them. Put in a couple of anchovy fillets (from a jar) into each half pepper plus some chopped up garlic. Pour olive oil over and shove in to the oven. Cook until they are soft. Serve the peppers individually on a plate on top of a bed of mixed salad leaves or baby spinach (having first mixed the salad with a good olive oil, a drop of balsamic vinegar and a teaspoon of maple syrup.) It makes a splendid first course or buffet dish.

Liz's variation is to chop up a bit of goat's cheese and add to each plate.

Charles' variation is to put a couple of baby tomatoes in each half pepper when roasting them in the oven. He also leaves out the salad, preferring the peppers to sit alone on the plate (preferably a white one) so that their contrasting colours stand out better.

Helene Hanff
WRITER

Yorkshire pudding

Darling James,

Of course you can use Cecily's Yorkshire Pudding recipe from *84 Charing Cross Road*. I'm sure she'd be as flattered as I am to be in such distinguished company. I add a variation I've made to the recipe for cooks in England as addicted to special Sunday breakfasts as we are over here. If you cook sausages for Sunday breakfast, put the Yorkshire pudding in as usual, using sausage grease in place of roast beef dripping. I personally find the pudding is better that way - especially with maple syrup (our version of treacle) poured over it and the sausages at the table. Fans have told me, by the way, that short-order cooks can use Bisquick[†] in place of flour, it's foolproof.

[†] *(American instant baking mix)*

Cecily:

Helene, my dear,

There are many ways of doing it but Mummy and I think this is the simplest for you to try. Put a cup of flour, an egg, half a cup of milk, and a good shake of salt into a large bowl and beat all together until it is the consistency of thick cream. Put in the fridge for several hours. It's best if you make it in the morning. When you put your roast in the oven, put in an extra pan to heat. Half an hour before your roast is done, pour a bit of the roast grease into the baking pan, just enough to cover the bottom will do. The pan must be very hot. Now pour the pudding in and the roast and the pudding will be ready at the same time. I don't quite know how to describe it to someone who has never seen it, but a good Yorkshire pudding will puff up very high and brown and crisp, and when you cut into it you will find that it is hollow inside. The RAF is still keeping Doug in Norfolk and we are firmly hoarding your Christmas tins until he comes home, but, oh, my dear, what a celebration we shall have when he does! I do think you oughtn't to spend your money like that. Must fly and post this if you're going to have it in time for Brian's birthday dinner. Do let me know if it's a success.

Love, Cecily.

Helene:

Dear Cecily,

Yorkshire Pudding out of this world! We have nothing like it. I had to describe it to someone as a high, curved, smooth, empty waffle.

Best, Helene.

The Countess of **Harewood**

Barbecue

Having been born and bred in Australia, I have a rather more relaxed approach to the barbecue than most inhabitants of these islands. Australians will barbecue anything at the drop of an Akubra (providing the summer fire bans are not in force) and I have had many delicious picnics cooked by the following two simple methods, one for the beach, the other really for anywhere at all. For the beach Barbie, set the children to gather anything which will burn - twigs, dried seaweed, paper, etc. Using the well-known boy scout trick of licking your finger and holding it in the air, determine the wind direction. Then scoop a hole about a foot deep in the sand with a sloping 'entrance' to it - about a foot long will do and it must face the wind. Build your fire in the hole and, when it is crackling merrily, cook your meat in a folding grill over it. The second method needs only an old kerosene tin and some newspaper. Screw the newspaper into tight little 'logs', put them into the bottom of the tin, light and cook as before with your folding grill. It works even better if you puncture the bottom of the tin. We have often had 'kerosene tin' picnics in the woods at Harewood, but I have yet to venture one on an English beach!

Nick Hopkins
DEPUTY FOREIGN EDITOR, THE GUARDIAN

Peach crunch

Long before chocolate bars were being deep fried, and before mudpies were being baked in the name of Mississippi, a pudding was doing the round of households around the suburbs of London that I suspect has played a small but not insignificant part in current concerns about the level of societal obesity. My mother called it 'Peach Crunch'. This it certainly did on the day of making. But the longer it kept the harder it got, so it was important - so my mother reasoned - to eat as much of it as possible as quickly as possible. Calorie counters should look away now. There are several key elements to a successful Peach Crunch. Golden syrup is a must for the chocolatey cornflake base. There's no point shirking on the double cream either. And fresh peaches simply won't do for the decoration on top. An essential compliment to the pudding is, you see, the syrupy juice that comes with the tinned fruit. Each slice deserves a dribble. Disgusting, you say? Maybe. But I offer this in defence.'I used to slave away in the kitchen before dinner parties, making elaborate mousses and things like that,' sighed my mother. 'And when our friends arrived, the men would always whisper to me, 'You have made the Peach Crunch, haven't you?''

The recipe
4oz cooking chocolate
4oz butter
3 tablespoons Golden Syrup
4oz icing sugar

6-8oz cornflakes

½ pint double cream

I tin of sliced peaches

Melt the chocolate and butter in a saucepan, stirring in the Golden Syrup. When all melted, add the icing sugar. Beat it in well and fold the mix into cornflakes with a wooden spoon, then put in a flat dish. Press it down evenly. Whip the cream and spread it on top of the cornflakes. Decorate the top with tinned peaches.

Anthony Horowitz
AUTHOR AND SCREENWRITER

My mother's turkey soup

My mother, who died twelve years ago, was a quite wonderful cook. As I am writing this at the end of the festive season, let me give you her recipe for turkey soup. Remove all the flesh from the carcass of your (large, free range) turkey but leave the skin. Break up the carcass and bake in a high oven for twenty minutes - until brown. Cover with water in a saucepan and gently boil for the whole morning. Strain off the liquid - this is the soup. Now fry carrots, celery and fine barley in a pan. Add the stock and boil for two hours.

I particularly remember this soup as my mother unfortunately slipped and poured a bowl of it all over me when I was recovering from a bad dose of flu. The result was a map of Africa on my chest and stomach. It took a month for the scald marks to heal. But the flu was cured instantly. My mother considered this to be something of a triumph.

Angela Huth
NOVELIST AND PLAYWRIGHT

Goats cheese soufflé

When I was married to Quentin Crewe, in the early Sixties, he was not yet the famous food writer he was to become. But he was already a restaurant critic and therefore, to anyone who undertook to cook for him, something of a challenge. When we moved to a house in Bedfordshire we were lucky enough to acquire the very best of English cooks, Mrs Eaton, commonly known as Edgy, who insisted we pay her no more than £6 a week. Out of her £8 a week housekeeping she managed to buy many pieces of kitchen equipment, as well as vast amounts of food, so her husbandry was as good as her cooking. She was happiest when we filled the house: twelve to every meal she saw as ideal, and something that should be frequently repeated. We often had to disappoint her.

Edgy saw no reason to lower her standards when we were on our own in the week. One evening we sat in the library awaiting her famous goat's cheese soufflé. She came in without it to announce, calmly, there was a fierce fire in the outhouse next to the kitchen. Quentin rushed to ring the fire engine. 'You can't possibly do that,' Edgy said, 'the soufflé's not ready. I can't have firemen running about till it's out of the oven.' She was adamant. Never has there been a longer eight minutes, while we imagined the flames beginning to devour the house, till she reappeared with a perfect, quivering soufflé. Only then was Quentin permitted to dial 999. It may have been the speed and the alarm with which we ate that made it the most remarkable soufflé of my life, and the firemen, their work swiftly done, joined us for hedgehog pudding.

The recipe
14oz goat's cheese
2oz flour
2oz butter
salt, pepper, fresh or dried thyme
¼ pt of milk
6 eggs
Make a roux, adding more milk if too stiff. Let boil for a minute then add chopped cheese, seasoning and thyme. Separate eggs. When cheese mixture is cool, add yolks one at a time. Whisk whites stiffly, fold in. Pour into buttered dish and cook in a moderate oven for approximately 30 minutes, when the soufflé should be well risen but slightly soft in the centre.

David Inshaw

ARTIST

A breakfast for Ruralists

For several years the Brotherhood of Ruralists spent every autumn holiday at Combe Valley near Morwenstow in Cornwall. We all used to eat communally, even employing a cook as our holiday numbers grew from year to year, and we wanted time for painting. As you can imagine, we had some great meals in wonderful company. But the best of all was what became known as the Great Ruralist Breakfast. It all started when, after arriving at our cottage late one very wet night, without provisions, we had to make do the next morning with what the local shop had to offer, a few sausages and a tin of beans. This was all right but we decided to add a new ingredient the following morning. And eggs were included. The next day, bacon; the following morning, mushrooms; then tomatoes, and black puddings; and because it's Cornwall, we found a shop selling white pudding. Fried bread and kidneys were added at some point, and by now it was taking almost all the morning to prepare, eat and clear away! This was all right because it rained almost all of that holiday.

The final ingredient came towards the end of this holiday when we found some shaggy parasols, a rather large mushroom which grew on the cliff near our cottage. These are enormous. By now our plates were groaning under the weight. But we did enjoy those breakfasts more than any others I have had. You have to be a real expert to prepare, fry and keep warm all that lot ready to serve! As we built up gradually to this final meal we didn't feel any sense of over-eating or indulgence, and during the afternoons on the beach or the cliffs, we soon worked it off.

We took it in turns to cook. In the cottage were Peter Blake, Chrissy Wilson, Robin and myself. Friends came and stayed and went away feeling very satisfied. The other Ruralists, such as Graham and Ann Ovenden, and Graham and Ann Arnold, stayed in other cottages, but I don't know what they did for their breakfast.

PS. In 1985 I became a vegetarian and I do miss sausages above all.

Moyshe Kalman
NATUROPATH

Hollishkes

Since our marriage, my wife and I have made a journey from the fat and refined carbohydrates which have traditionally marked our Jewish diet. We have wholeheartedly embarked upon adapting a really wholefood and healthy diet to those rules we hold to be spiritually healthy. Through all of this journey, one old favourite, Hollishkes, has still remained high on our list of the top ten. 'Hollishke' is an Eastern European word but the dish is often called by a more descriptive Yiddish name, 'Gefilte Kraut' - plain old stuffed cabbage. The dish is eaten two times in the year on Festive occasions, and its symbolism has always amused and appealed to us. During the High Holy Days when our souls are under close scrutiny from above, we refrain from eating foods (leaf vegetables) which themselves require close inspection for insects, the consumption of which are strictly forbidden by our Dietary Laws. When the last day arrives, and the pressure is off a bit, Hollishkes are served as a means of demonstrating this relief. The second time we eat Hollishkes is on Purim, a delightful minor festival just before the Passover. Legend has it that on Purim, not being an important festival, housewives were admonished to conceal the meat and not make the bigger festivals jealous! We suspect that this clever way of stretching meat with inexpensive ingredients really reflects the crushing poverty our ancestors endured for centuries. Whatever the excuse for the dish, it's great.

The recipe

2 medium cabbages (about 3½ lb, each)

1½ lbs meat

3 large onions grated

3 tablespoons rice

8ozs tomato purée

Juice of two lemons

Salt, pepper, sugar to taste.

Blanche cabbage and remove leaves. Mix meat, 3 tablespoons onions, pepper, 2 tablespoons purée, and rice. Place a tablespoon of this mixture on 20-22 leaves and fold. Mix rest of ingredients with a little water and boil. Place remainder of leaves in the bottom of a large pot and pile up the Hollishkes, cover with water and boil 6-8 hours.

Penelope Keith
ACTOR

Chunky orange marmalade

It is mid-January and I have just finished my third batch of marmalade. The house smells deliciously orangey, and the top shelf of the larder is groaning under the weight of about two dozen full jars of various sizes. After being disappointed with nearly all the commercial brands of marmalade (the fruit content seemed to get less and less as the price went up) I tried various recipes and eventually looked in my oldest cookbook (no glossy photos and everything in pounds and ounces, bought in the sixties for 2/11d) and found this one. I have used it for nearly twenty years and I commend it to you.

The recipe
4*lb* Seville oranges
2 sweet oranges
2 lemons
6pints water
6*lb* sugar
Wash fruit thoroughly. Put in pan with water and simmer slowly until tender enough to pierce with a fork. This takes approximately one hour. Take off heat and allow to cool. Remove the fruit, but leave the water in the pan. Cut fruit in half and remove pips and pith. Then shred and slice the skin, not too fine or the marmalade will not be chunky. Return the cut-up fruit to the pan with the water in which the oranges were cooked, stir in the sugar, bring to the boil. Simmer moderately fast until a little of it will set when tested. Pot whilst hot.

Francis King
NOVELIST

Liver and bacon

When I am alone, my favourite dish - ideal for a bachelor always in a hurry - is liver and bacon. The thinly sliced liver only has to be dredged with seasoned flour and fried for two or three minutes in hot olive oil. Bacon is one of the few foods that are better cooked in a microwave oven than in a pan or under a grill. With mashed potato, the grilled halves of two tomatoes, a wedge of lemon and dollop of Dijon mustard, this is perfection for me.

My love of liver dates back to the last war - when, like some bird bent on feeding its clamorous nestlings, my widowed mother would tirelessly scavenge London for food for her three children. One of the best sources was Bellamy's, a firm of butchers going back to the 18th century, now sadly vanished from its premises near the conjunction between Earls Court Road and High Street Kensington. Here usually in charge was a rotund man with hairy, tattooed forearms, red cheeks and a wreath of grey hair curling around a bald pate. My mother, pretty and indomitably cheerful, was a favourite of his. For her he always had something, most often liver, to produce from under the counter, with some comment to reassure any other customers present that it was either unrationed or fit only for animal consumption. She would complain to us of his 'cheeky' - by which she meant flirtatious - manner, and would then add something like 'Well, I suppose I'll just have to put up with it.' On one occasion I accompanied her into the shop, 'There you are my dear!' he said, holding out the package of liver. As she took it, he then raised a beefy, bloodstained hand and ran it down her cheek. My mother at once recoiled, then straightened and gave a smile that was almost a grimace. 'Something for your lovely little pussy,' he said. Neither my mother nor I, both innocents, suspected any *double entendre*. But I have often wondered since.

Jane Lapotaire
ACTOR AND WRITER

Tuna-fish and horseradish sandwich

It's not much of a recipe - considering how guilty I am of the sin of pride as a cook (I blame it all on a French grandmother who I never met, Marie Josephe Fredouelle) - it's only a sandwich filling! But it comes from a very memorable time in my life.

I was coping as a very new single mother, going through a divorce which I had instigated but in my heart of hearts didn't want. My son was six, coping with a new school in a foreign country and I was playing Piaf on Broadway. I had the luxury of only doing the seven performances a week, as the 'understudy' (a good actress in her own right) played the first matinee of the week, the Thursday, and I played the Saturday and the Sunday ones, and the four other shows of course.

Luxury two - I had a limousine! The first (and only) one of my life. The very first drive, a garbage truck went into the back of us in the Lincoln Tunnel. I bounced off the glass partition; the driver cut his head on the windscreen. The police closed the tunnel while we waited for another car. And all the driver kept saying in his best Brooklynese was, 'I'm gonna sue, lady. Whaddyoo gonnado? I'm gonna sue!' I missed the dress rehearsal in Philadelphia, ended up with a blinding headache when I finally did get on stage that evening, and have whiplash which is with me to this day. I shouldda sooed. Don't cry stinking fish? Well that's exactly what I'm going to do.

Ever in the running for the good mother of the year award, I used to get up each morning about 7am, make my son's lunch box, have a very befuddled breakfast and then walk him down to the end of the block - West 13th between 6th and 7th, where we would wait for the school bus to pick him up. I valued this precious time together as I wouldn't see him for more than a rushed half hour at the end of his school day. This so-called quality time was very seriously undermined by him developing a somewhat quirky New York taste - tuna fish and horseradish sandwiches. That's it. Mix a little creamed horseradish into the tuna, slap it on some bread of your choice with salad, and hey presto. Having been gutted by Piaf the night before, I used to chant at him, 'Greater love hath no mother than to face a tuna fish sandwich at seven in the morning.'

Laurie Lee
AUTHOR

Bouillabaisse

I thought you must be pulling my leg when you asked me to send you a recipe - me, the great egg-on-toast man, but here is one of my favourite recipes, bouillabaisse. This great fish dish of the French Mediterranean - particularly the area surrounding Marseilles - is best prepared and cooked by local fishermen from a catch they have freshly landed. It is also, perhaps, best eaten out of doors, during a slow but midsummer afternoon with pastis, wine and gossip, and nothing else to do for the rest of the day.

I first tasted bouillabaisse under the shade of pine trees by a shining estuary near the fishing town of Martigues. My wife's relations and friends were all fishermen from the town, and they tied up their boat by a small wooden cabin where they seemed to keep all that was necessary for comfort. The preparation of the meal was leisured and devoted - fish sorted and cleaned, crustaceans well scrubbed, fennel, saffron, and bread chopped up and arranged, and pastis screwed deep in a tub of ice.

We had gathered at noon. The stew was boiled in a great iron pot hanging over a fire of blazing pine twigs. A man took an hour stirring the garlic sauce, another arguing and giving advice. After its long steady simmering and slow mixing of juices, the meal was served up in deep copper bowls. It tasted of Provence, high summer, and all the treasures of the sea, and we spread the luxury of eating it over several hours, then slept on warm beds of pine needles and only woke at last to the chapel bell ringing for vespers.

The recipe

Fish needed: sole, John Dory, monkfish, red mullet, conger eel, bass whiting, turbot, rock salmon. All or some of these fish can be used according to taste and availability.

Method

Put into a saucepan 3 sliced onions, 4 crushed garlic cloves, 2 peeled potatoes, a sprig of thyme, a bay leaf. Place the firm fish on top (monkfish, red mullet, conger eel, turbot) and pour over half a small wine glass of olive oil, and cover all with boiling water. Season with salt, pepper and saffron, and boil fast. After five minutes add the soft fish (whiting, bass, sole, plaice, John Dory) and boil another five to ten minutes. Remove from fire. A few cockles and small shellfish and prawns can be added. Make *aïoli*, stiff mayonnaise with garlic. Put half of this into the bouillabaisse. Keep the rest as a dip.

Make *rouille* sauce also for a dip: take one large garlic clove, 2 or 3 chilis, and pound in a mortar adding small drops of olive oil till a thick paste forms. Add a slice of boiled potato and a yolk of a hard boiled egg (sea urchin eggs are a good addition), add some of the bouillabaisse sauce and a little vinegar.

Put cooked fish on a separate dish. Make some rounds of French bread toasts and place in another dish and pour the liquid over them. Sprinkle the fish with parsley and serve all together. Add the sauces to your own taste.

The *rouille* is a hot sauce which makes a nice contrast to the blander mayonnaise. Sometimes the toasts are served crisp and separate and can be dipped into the *aïoli* and *rouille*.

Rula Lenska
ACTOR

Snuffles

My Mama was not a great cook, and as children we were not very fond of traditional Polish food - lots of pickled vegetables, carp which I personally think is a revolting fish, and *Kluski* which are a variation of dumplings and noodles. However Mama did become very adept at making delicious little starter snacks which always looked and tasted quite glamorous, yet were very quick and very cheap to make. This particular one was a great favourite at parties and people always asked for the recipe.

The recipe
Ingredients
6oz Philadephia cheese
6oz Campbell's beef consommé
I squashed clove of garlic
Pinch of curry powder

Blend all the ingredients in a blender, add some dry sherry and parsley, turn into small ramekins and chill. Serve with thin strips of toasted rye bread or celery sticks.

Yum, Yum...thank you, Mama!

Lady **Livsey** of Talgarth

Pasta with asparagus and Parmesan

Third time lucky...
Being very fond of asparagus, I was very keen to have an asparagus bed and finally established one - then we moved house! At the new house I planted a second asparagus bed - and again we moved house! When I started to plant one in our new home near Brecon the family said, 'No, Mum, we will only move house again!' However, the asparagus bed is now well established and we enjoy the crop each year.

The recipe (Serves 4-6)
1 onion, finely chopped
14oz thin asparagus
2oz butter
3fl oz dry white wine
14oz dried pasta (e.g. Spirals)
10fl oz double cream
Salt and pepper
2oz Parmesan cheese, grated

Cut asparagus into two inch lengths and blanch in boiling water for 2-3 minutes until tender. Reserve 5 tablespoons of the blanching water. Melt the butter and cook onion until soft. Add asparagus, reserved blanching water and the wine. Cook until most of the liquid has evaporated. Cook the pasta in boiling salted water until *al dente*. Drain. Add the cream to the sauce and stir well. Heat gently until bubbling. Stir in half the cheese, taste and season. Toss the sauce into the pasta. Serve with remaining Parmesan sprinkled over.

John McCarthy
JOURNALIST

Shepherd's pie

Shepherd's pie was always a favourite during my childhood. Throughout autumn and winter it was one of my mother's regular offerings. Served with sprouts or greens, I still love it because it brings back the comfortable atmosphere of happy family evenings with my parents and brother. On a cold evening there is nothing like it.

The recipe
1 large onion, chopped
1*lb* minced beef
Large tin chopped tomatoes
Tomato purée
1*tsp* horseradish sauce
Sprinkling dried mixed herbs
Small tin baked beans
2*lb* potatoes for mashed topping

Sauté the onion in a frying pan until clear and then transfer it to a casserole. Fry the mince until browned and add to onions, discarding most of the fat. Add the tinned tomatoes, a couple of tablespoons of purée, the horse radish sauce, herbs, and season well with salt and pepper, and stir well. Put the covered casserole in the middle of the oven at 190^C for about half an hour. Try the meat sauce and add more herbs and seasoning to taste. Stir in the baked beans and return casserole to oven. Have the potatoes on the boil and, when cooked, mash them. Get grill hot, remove casserole from oven and spread potatoes over sauce and place under grill until nicely browned. Sometimes I add a little grated cheese as a final topping.

Clare Margetson
EDITOR - WOMEN'S SECTION, THE GUARDIAN

Nigella's blueberry muffins

Like most people who get home late from work, starving, and then spend the weekend catching up on sleep and friends (that was pre-children) or reacquainting yourself with your baby (how it is now), my cooking has been somewhat restricted. I find it mostly comes down to the quickest of pastas (pesto 5 minutes, tomato sauce 10), or sausages and mash. That's not to say I don't like cooking - I really do. Finding the time is the problem.

So when Nigella Lawson hit the scene with her domestic goddess tag, I too ignored any possible irony involved and snarled at the absurd, antiquated notion that women should get back to their baking trays. What, work all day, come home, sort the washing, pay the bills, fix dinner, oh, AND bake muffins for breakfast? Then I got pregnant. And something deeply hormonal kicked in that made me want to bake as if my growing baby's life depended on it. It happened the first time. And it's happening again now. Laundry piles up and bills come in red, but it's OK, because the house is infused with cooking smells. I could pretend I am following the example of Sylvia Plath, who baked while awaiting inspiration. But for me, I think it has been more to do with my lion-like appetite.

So this is the recipe I find easiest and most totally delicious. It doesn't take long at all, but the results are impressive. Just make sure you don't come over too domestic goddessly smug...

The recipe

75g unsalted butter

200g plain flour

½ teaspoon bicarbonate soda

2 teaspoons baking powder

75g caster sugar

Pinch of salt

200ml buttermilk (or 100g yoghurt and 100ml milk)

1 large egg

200g blueberries

Heat the oven to 200°C Gas Mark 6. Melt the butter, then let it cool while you mix the dry ingredients in a bowl (flour, bicarb, baking powder, sugar, salt). In a jug beat together the buttermilk, egg and butter. Pour the wet mixture into the dry and mix gently with a wooden spoon. Don't overwork it, and don't worry too much about lumps. Fold in the fruit. Add (possibly) a touch of orange zest. Then spoon into 12 paper cases in a baking tray and bake for 20 minutes until golden on top.

Sir **John Margetson**

English trifle

Anglo-Dutch defence relations did not rest entirely on my wife's trifle, but it made a contribution. On many occasions, in my capacity as ambassador to the Hague, we entertained the Dutch Chief of Defence Staff to dinner. The first time he came Miranda gave him trifle. Thereafter, he always asked as he arrived, 'Is it trifle tonight?' It always was when he came. This pudding, much neglected or else ruined by ignorance or incompetence, is, when well made, one of the glories of English cooking. Forget the travesties of trifles served in many restaurants and for sale in supermarkets. Here is our recipe for the real thing.

The recipe and method
Cut up some home-made sponge cake and line a large glass dish with it. Sprinkle it liberally with sherry. Then cover it with a layer of dried apricots, which have been cooked beforehand and turned into a rough purée. Take a handful of *amaretti* biscuits. Crush them into coarse pieces and sprinkle them on the apricots. On top of that put a thick layer of home-made custard (made with a pint of creamy milk, plenty of egg yolks, a few drops of genuine vanilla extract, and a good teaspoon of cornflour.) Cover it all with a generous layer of whipped cream. Finally take a handful of slivered almonds. Brown them in a dry pan or in the oven. Scatter them casually over the top and add no further decoration.

Christopher Matthew
AUTHOR

Suleiman's Pilaff

In 1982, my old friend Benny Green and I published an annotated edition of *Three Men in A Boat*. By the time we had finished tiddling round the Thames and rummaging in history books, there was not a single reference to which we had not come up with an explanation or on which we had not expanded. Historical characters and events, newspaper stories of the day, architectural curiosities, clothing, comic songs, camping equipment, shops, pubs - you name it, we wrote about it. Thanks in no small part to Benny's wise, witty and constantly entertaining company, it was as enjoyable a literary enterprise as I have ever undertaken.

That summer, Benny and I and Tim Rice (who happened to be our publisher as well as friend) were persuaded by a BBC producer called Richard Denton to recreate Jerome K. Jerome's famous river journey from Kingston-upon-Thames to Oxford for a documentary film wittily entitled *Three More Men in a Boat*. The idea was to row a bit (in an authentic 19th century camping skiff), talk a lot - about the book and how life on the river had changed in a hundred years - visit some of the places that Jerome K. Jerome's three men - George, Harris and the narrator - visited in 1888, and have a few adventures of our own. Montmorency, the dog, was played by Tim's lovely old boxer, Bonzo, and Benny brought his saxophone along to serenade us in quieter moments.

Benny entered into the proceedings with somewhat less enthusiasm than Tim and me -

partly because he hadn't a clue how to row and had never learned to swim, but mainly because he refused to spend a night under canvas in the skiff. He abandoned us twice during the course of the filming. The first time was in the dark, somewhere near Sonning, just as Tim and I were struggling to erect the canvas cover by the dim light of a tiny gas lamp. He did it again somewhere in the middle of nowhere as I was attempting in the cool of the evening to re-create the Irish stew which our heroes cooked over a wood fire beside the river and about which the narrator waxed so lyrical. 'I don't think I ever enjoyed a meal more. There was something fresh and piquant, a new flavour, with a taste like nothing else on earth.' The producer had provided us with some of the same ingredients: potatoes, carrots, peas, cold beef, an onion, and a couple of eggs - though not, I am glad to say, the remains of a pork pie, the bit of cold boiled bacon, and the tin of potted salmon that the original three chucked in for good measure. In the face of much scornful barracking from my two companions, I managed to get the vegetables boiling and had just started frying the onion, the beef and the eggs, when Benny announced he was off to find the nearest kosher Chinese restaurant and disappeared amidst a herd of cows. Tim was by now in less cheerful mood than he had been, and was less cheerful still when I stood up to move the picnic hamper and knocked over the saucepan, scattering the vegetables in every direction. As daylight faded, we picked gloomily at the meat and eggs and the few scraps of undercooked carrot we were able to rescue from the thick grass. And all the while, the camera kept turning. 'Sadly, there are so many ducks à l'orange within about ten yards of us,' Tim said gloomily. 'There are two fantastic dinners going down the river there.' If someone had thought to buy us oranges, we might have been sorely tempted.

I have often meant to cook *duck à l'orange* since that day. The nearest I got was the other day when I found a recipe in *The Times* for Marmalade Chicken. It's basically chicken legs and thighs, coated with a mixture of marmalade, mustard, salt, pepper, orange juice and olive oil. It was such a success with the family, I feel I am ready to move on to duck any day now.

Meanwhile, inspired by the three men's enthusiasm for using up leftovers, I can always fall back on a recipe that Auberon Waugh's wife invented by finishing off cold roast lamb. It's called Suleiman's Pilaff, and goes as follows:

The recipe
1lb cold roast lamb
2 onions
2oz butter
3oz sultanas
2oz pine nuts
4 small ground peppercorns
8oz rice
2 small cartons of yoghurt
2oz grated Parmesan.
Chop onions and melt in frying pan with butter. Add sultanas, pine nuts, rosemary, garlic, almonds, salt and pepper. Cook gently and add lamb chopped into small pieces. Cook rice in salted water, drain and add one carton of yoghurt, plus previously cooked ingredients, and half grated Parmesan. Serve piping hot with some yoghurt on the side and the remaining Parmesan. Serves four - or three in a boat, and a dog. It's as good as Irish stew any day.

Self-Sufficiency (after Growing Up)

I've got a book called 'Catering for Singles';
And lots of cookery cards with ring-holes;
I'm a widower who'd like to win girls;
Who's coming home with me?

My chef d'oeuvre is *entrecôte Béarnaise*
With haricots verts and a few pommes Lyonnaises
As for my spaghetti Bolognese -
What can I say? Wowee!

I'm as inventive as Gary or Jamie;
And, if I dare say so, who could blame me?
No one in Frozen Foods would betray me;
And no one comes home with me.

Deborah Moggach
AUTHOR

By the beautiful blue Danube.

A few years ago I fell in love with a Hungarian. Soon I discovered that Hungarians don't come in ones; my house rapidly filled up with his various friends, friends of friends and relations of friends of friends, all arriving in London with nowhere to live and all wanting work. They were mostly young craftsmen - art students and sculptors - and so they set about renovating my house. As I paid them by the hour they worked well into the night and got terribly hungry. Feeding them all was quite a challenge, particularly because my boyfriend was a vegetarian. Not only vegetarian - he didn't eat courgettes, or peppers or aubergines. Nor anything pre-packaged, nor from a tin, though he happily swigged Coke (consis-tency was not his strong point). Nor did he like the way I fried onions or tomatoes. So I had to cook vast dishes of sturdy, nourishing, cheap food without certain vegetables in them. The following are two of my most reliable stand-bys. (Hungarian cuisine, by the way, is not great on vegetables - all meat and stodge. One of their few vegetarian dishes, and their most dispiriting, is spaghetti with jam.)

Potato and cabbage thing

This is dead easy. Butter a big ovenproof dish and layer it with thinly-sliced raw potatoes, masses of garlic, raw cabbage and thick slices of cheddar cheese. Season with salt and pepper and pour some milk over it (enough to come up about a third of the way), Brush the top layer of potatoes with oil. Put into a low oven for a long time - two hours maybe. This is surprisingly delicious, particularly the scabby brown bits round the edges and on top.

Carrot and butter bean soup

Soak some butter beans overnight. Fry some onions in a big saucepan, add the drained butter beans and some carrots, sliced. Add boiling water and a vegetable stock cube, plus a sprinkling of tarragon. Simmer until the beans are cooked - an hour or so - skimming the froth off the top. You can feed a lot of Hungarians for very little money with this soup, and it's very good. The tarragon makes the difference.

Mirabel Osler
AUTHOR

A salutary incident in the Pindus Mountains

Mirabel Osler is the author of 'A Gentle Plea for Chaos', 'In the Eye of the Garden', etc.

Having walked up from the river gully to air as clear and dry as a note of music, we found a taverna with chairs and a couple of round iron tables on a terrace overlooking a wilderness of juniper and arbutus. Weary and hungry, we ordered ouzo from the old woman who came out to greet us. We asked her if we could have something to eat: anything, please, whatever you have! 'We have this morning's eggs, sheep's cheese, fresh liver, fresh bread, tomato salad and wine.' We ordered bread, liver, salad, wine and cheese. Nightingales were singing in the green folds of the ravine, goat bells trailed through undergrowth on the opposite mountain flank and distantly eagles were circling the crags. Suspended in sunlight, bliss was in that moment until the old woman walked past with a goat on the end of a rope. Simultaneously we leapt up horrified. 'My God, not that fresh!' we said. 'Please, an omelette would be perfect.'

Jonathon Porritt
ENVIRONMENTAL CAMPAIGNER AND WRITER

Shelf sufficiency

Jonathon Porritt is Programme Director - Forum for the Future, and Chairman - UK Sustainable Development Commission.

For reasons that are far too complicated to go into here, I found myself about ten years ago staying in a remote cottage near Abergavenny with nothing to eat but stale white bread, streaky bacon several days past its sell-by-date and a pot of marmite. To which I was able to add a banana purchased that day at Paddington Station, but not consumed on the train. So I made a toasted sandwich combining the lot. Unbelievable. There was something about the innate aggression of the bacon that perfectly complemented the restfulness of the banana, just to get seriously pretentious about things. I have repeated the experiment many times since then, with other platforms apart from stale white bread and other 'melding agents' apart from marmite. Boursin is particularly recommended, especially for lovers of alliteration for whom the notion of a Bacon, Banana and Boursin Butty will delight the mind even as it tickles the taste buds!

Stanley Price
AUTHOR AND PLAYWRIGHT

Grandma White's recipe for 'original' Lithuanian chopped herring

My maternal grandmother, escaping the 1880's pogroms in Lithuania, which was then part of Russia, set sail for Ireland, or maybe it was New York, but got off in Cork. (Well, it does sound a bit like New York, especially if you don't speak English.) She was probably about 16. She complained to the captain about the attentions of a young man, who was told to leave her alone. Three months later, the family story goes, she met him again at a tea party in Dublin and shortly afterwards married him. Apparently she was beautiful and cooked just like his mother. In fact any East European Jewish woman would have cooked pretty much like his mother. The dishes were traditional, only differentiated by the subtlest addition of an ingredient or the sheer expertise of the cook. My mother, born and brought up in Dublin and apparently untouched by Irish cuisine, brought the recipes to London - in her head, of course. I prevailed on her to write them down. Grandma White's chopped herring, amongst other things, had to be preserved for posterity.

The recipe
1 jar of Bismark herrings, preferably Mrs Elwood's
Some onion from the herring marinade
2 eating apples
2 hard-boiled eggs
1 level tablespoon sugar

Squeeze herrings as dry as possible. Skin them. Chop and add apples and one egg, pepper and sugar to taste. Blend in food processor, or by hand if you are a purist. The mixture should look chopped but not liquidised. Spread onto a shallow plate or dish. Grate second egg on top of the herring mixture. Preferably eat with hard-baked water biscuits. Perfect with schnapps or vodka, but definitely not wine. It is a cure for all manner of ailments, including anti-semitism.

James Radcliff
CHAIRMAN - LAYTONS WINE MERCHANTS

Tales from the cellar

Over 40 years in the Wine Trade has given one many memories. In the main happy. The opportunity to dine at some of the world's best restaurants, drink some of the very finest wines and to make great friendships.

Starting in the Wine Trade as an *étagère* in 1964, my initial baptism was working in the Cellars of Maison Lupe Cholet in Nuits St Georges. Burgundy has always had a great affection in my heart. Not only for the incomparable wines they produce, but also the people and stories arising.

I will never forget an evening in September 1964 - I was a cellar boy working in the aforementioned cellars in Nuits St Georges under the sponsorship of Christopher and Co - a firm that alas, has gone the way of all flesh - when the formidable figure of Comtesse Liane de Lupe Cholet, owner with her sister, Inez, of this highly respected Négociant, asked me to join her for dinner. I was terrified - her presence was not dissimilar to Florence Bates as the tiresome Mrs Van Hopper in Daphne du Mauriers *Rebecca*. I was told that we were going to one of the top restaurants in the Côte d'Or - just her and me. The Comtesse, a sophisticated and worldly lady and me - unsophisticated, 5 foot 9 inches tall, 9½ stone and still waiting for my growth spurt to start, about to enter into a culinary adventure I had only dreamt of. How was I going to cope with *cuisse de grenouille, escargot, boudin* etc? The answer was not well. There were lots of encouraging noises to try, as new to me as they were exotic.

'Une douzaine, escargots for Monsieur? - oui - merci'. Cold sweat began to develop whilst trying to make polite conversation and seeing what looked like instruments of torture being brought to the table, actually the *pince à escargots* looked as harmless as eye lash curlers. How on earth do they work? Some 10 minutes later - our first course was served. *Potage* for my hostess and a 'sizzling' *douzaine* for me - how unfair is that ?! Now what do I do? At this juncture I had no idea that I was never going to get past number 2 escargot. Number 1 was not a problem - I managed to ease out this revolting 'bogey'-like creature on a skewer and swallowed - 'Robert est votre Oncle!' With increased confidence I ventured to use the eyelash curlers - big mistake. I fixed my gaze on this particular *Helix Pomatia* and chased him around the *assiete d'escargots* dislodging his friends en route. Having finally caught the quarry and clasping him between the pincers, the sizzling hot shell ejected itself with great force - down the ample cleavage of my hostess. The resultant chaos was off the Richter scale. The Comtesse screamed and at the same time ejected herself with such force from her chair that the *Potage de Nuits* - the 1969 Nuits St Georges Chateau Gris, a bottle of Badoit and the remaining 11 molluscs departed from the table, along with the breadrolls and napkins. The relationship of the hostess with the management was such that I seem to remember we somehow how miraculously disappeared from the restaurant, and I to my small bedsit in Nuits St Georges pondering on the difficulties of learning by experience.

Some bottles I have loved

1962 Pommard

London Bottled - Christopher and Company

At a recent reunion I tasted this wine and it was still alive - in fact for ten minutes it stood up very well before collapsing. For me it was particularly interesting as I bottled it in the cellars in Sono. Burgundys from this era, when bottled in the UK, always seemed to have an interesting provenance, as often 'vin medicine' was added to give colour and weight. The 'medicine' wines were usually sourced from Algeria or northern Rhone and appeared without any reference to the Appellation Certificate. The price? a mere 7 shillings a bottle! - sorry - 35p.

1976 Sancerre 'Mont Damnes'

Domaine Cotat à Chavignol

Drank two years ago. Who would think a 26-year-old Sancerre was still as perky as ever. Very pale in colour - reminiscent of Condrieu. The most surprising element was the sweetness on the finish. The very hot summer had produced very ripe grapes leaving a certain amount of residual sugar on the finished wine. Paul Cotat was a minimal interventionist. Clarified his wines and bottled the wines only when there was a full moon - something about the gravitational pull ensuring a 'bright wine'.

1945 Fleurie *Paul Sapin*

Emile Brousseloux discovered that his late father had bricked up part of his cellar in Lancie in the Beaujolais in 1944 to hide from the occupiers a quantity of his best village Beaujolais. You're right, although it was labelled 1945 it can't have been. Suffice to say that it was older, and what was amazing, it was fine if you could drink it within three minutes of opening !

Fiona Reynolds
DIRECTOR GENERAL OF THE NATIONAL TRUST

Cushiony biscuits

This is a recipe from my childhood, which has continued into my childen's. I'm one of five sisters, and we used to go on holiday with another family, who had three girls. We were very close and shared many wet camping and walking holidays in the Lake District and Snowdonia. We all loved these biscuits, which were made by our friends' mother, Aunty Miriam, and a tin of them wooed us to the tops of cloudy mountains and on endless walks to look at waterfalls in the rain. She was eventually persuaded to give us the recipe, and it still works a treat today for my own three daughters. I don't know where the name came from, but I have a vague memory of us trying to describe why we liked them so much, the answer being that they were, well, cushiony... Try them, they are!

The recipe
12oz self raising flour
8oz caster sugar
4oz butter or margarine
3oz (about 3 tablespoons) Golden Syrup
I egg
I *tsp* bicarbonate of soda
I *tsp* ginger

Mix dry ingredients together in a bowl. Melt the butter/margarine and syrup in a pan. Add the beaten egg and melted butter/syrup to dry ingredients - it should form a soft mixture. Using your hands, roll the mixture into balls the size of large marbles, flatten the tops gently and place on greased baking trays (not too close together, they will spread). Cook for about 10 minutes at 160°C Gas Mark 4. Remove from the baking tray to cool. They should be soft and cushiony with a slight crunch when cool. Practice makes perfect in getting the texture just right!

Lady **Anya Sainsbury**

Just dessert

*Lady Sainsbury
is a former
ballerina, and
founder of
The Linden Trust*

The following recipe was invented spontaneously by John, fairly early in our marriage. We were down at our lovely weekend house in Kent, built for us a few years before by Hugh Casson, overlooking Romney Marsh. John offered to make a pudding for a meal. He knew we had bought some brandy snaps and wanted to fill them with whipped cream: simple and delicious. I was next door in the sitting room, reading a story to one of the children and heard this mad whipping going on next door in our kitchen/ dining room and then groans and the odd curse, and I realised that the cream was not whipping. Not to be defeated, John crushed up the brandy snaps, threw them into the cream, sloshed a lot of brandy in, mixed it all together and put it in the freezer. Hey presto! A rather wonderful boozy pudding! I confess that though it seemed rather a triumph at the time, we have not tried it again, so it might need somebody to tinker with this recipe!

Norman Scarfe and **Paul Fincham**
HISTORIAN   WRITER

Supper for the Princess

The voice on the other end of the telephone had a slightly frantic note: 'We have Princess Margaret staying, unexpectedly, for the weekend. Could you both come and have a drink tomorrow evening?' Norman was out when this happened, but I remembered that when, a few months earlier, he'd had dinner with these same friends, when the Princess had been there too, she had, as he left, suggested that when next in Suffolk she might come and visit him at home. This seemed the right moment to make a counter-suggestion, which was taken up enthusiastically. The following evening the Princess arrived, with her host and hostess, not for a drink but for supper. Her two bodyguards made themselves at home in the study, asking only to be warned when the party was ready to leave. The five of us repaired to the sitting-room, before going in to eat. I'd quizzed Norman, after that earlier dinner-party, about HRH's appetite. He recalled mainly that she'd pushed some lamb chops around her plate several times before leaving most of them. But that was on 2nd June, the anniversary of the Coronation, and she was anxious to watch a film of the original occasion, on TV that evening; so everyone hurried through the meal to be in time for the programme. During it, eyes and ears tended to be on the Princess as much as on the film. When Dimbleby referred to the crown having to be remodelled slightly, she described a shape with her hands and murmured, almost to herself: 'Yes of course - Papa's head was that shape, but Liliibet is this shape'. It was touching; she loved re-living the big moment in her family's life. We decided to play for safety with a recipe I'd once culled from a newspaper where it was described as, 'so delicious and so simple that one is angry not to have thought of it for oneself'. It never fails to please our guests. On this occasion Princess Margaret delighted us by asking for (almost commanding) a second helping. The party stayed for three hours; conversation never flagged. When she reached for her handbag, I alerted the guards who dashed out to the cars. 'Delicious meal', said HRH as she shook my hand. And, as they drove home, the comment reported to us was: 'What a nice relaxed evening'. During it, she cheerfully committed herself to a book-launch at Bury St Edmunds, celebrating the 1944 Normandy landing on Sword Beach, led by the intrepid Ist Battalion The Suffolk Regiment, of which she was Colonel-in-Chief. This is what we ate. Quantities here are for four, but are easily expanded.

The recipe
4 large fresh eggs
4 slices of smoked salmon
4oz smoked cod's roe
4oz double cream or crème fraîche
Cook the eggs in boiling water for six minutes, then remove and cool in cold water for a couple of hours before peeling. This prevents the soft-boiled yolk from bursting through the white. Place each egg on a slice of smoked salmon. Skin the cod's roe and, preferably in a blender, beat it till smooth. Add the cream gradually, to make a kind of thick and delicious sauce to pour over the eggs, letting it run down decoratively on to the salmon. Sprinkle with chopped parsley or dill and garnish with a wedge of lemon. Brown bread-and-butter triangles complement it nicely and make sure that no sauce is left on the plate. You see why the Princess asked for more.

Ned Sherrin CBE
WRITER, DIRECTOR AND PERFORMER

Dear Jimmie,

I don't have any funny cooking stories. One early disaster (occurred?) when I was living in a room in Kenneth Fortescue's flat in Chelsea and attempted to make baked beans (also toast). The toast went well, but my preferred way of cooking baked beans was to immerse the tin, unopened, in boiling water and return to my room. The resulting explosion splattered the walls and ceiling. I'm better now!

Melisa Treasure

Monsieur Nibbles aux Pruneaux

During the long, hot summer of 1987, I was reading peacefully in the large garden of a boys' boarding house at Harrow School where my husband was a housemaster. It was during the holidays and the hill was deserted. Suddenly, Mr Nibbles, our children's rabbit, lolloped by, escaped from his compound! I leapt to my bare feet and, wearing only a tiny green bikini and a floppy straw hat, set off in hot pursuit, but he made for the woods. I would need shoes and something to catch him with: a large pair of knee-high black Wellington boots lay on the back doorstep and there was a rotting butterfly net in the shed: these would do at a pinch. So off I went, racing after Mr Nibbles, slamming the net down, but rather inaccurately, fearing I might mash him or cut him in two. This went on for some time, in and out of cold frames, round the huge foxes' earth, until our houseguest, Mark, an American publisher, arrived back from his game of tennis. To avoid the carcinogenic rays of the sun, he was wearing a drooping cotton hat, sunglasses, a long-sleeved shirt, the longest shorts, the tallest socks, and Keds, and a large dab of suncream on his nose- all white, of course. Only his knobbly pink knees spoilt the ensemble. Seeing my plight, he began threatening Mr Nibbles with his Slazenger racquet, but soon realised that this was useless. He disappeared into the garage and returned with a large brown supermarket box. Together, I in my wellies, bikini and hat, he in his whites, we pounded after Mr Nibbles who was clearly tireless, and had, by now, taken to the air, the

Nureyev of the cony world! Mark attempted, quite skilfully I thought, to field him in the cardboard box several times and I swept him into the net, but out he sprang, pirouetting across the garden and into the greenhouse which had so many broken windows that it was no use slamming the door. Finally I cornered him with my hat and Mark slammed the box down over Mr Nibbles with all his might! Now what? Here is a short recipe...

The method
Dust a jointed rabbit with seasoned flour and brown in butter. Remove rabbit to a casserole with 12 soaked and pitted prunes, 300*ml* (½*pt*) good stock, 300*ml* (½*pt*) red or white wine, bouquet garni, salt and pepper. Cover tightly and simmer for about two hours until the rabbit is tender. To finish add a glass of port, 75*gm* (3*oz*) each of currants and sultanas and simmer for a further 10 minutes. Sprinkle generously with parsley and serve with triangles of bread fried in butter. Sauté some sliced Mr Nibbles in butter for 10 minutes. Add salt and pepper and a glass of white wine and boil for 2 minutes. Add 3*oz* of double cream mixed with a teaspoon of flour. Stir till it reaches the boil and remove from flame. Serve with a purée of any root vegetable or beetroot.

Oliver Walston
BROADCASTER, WRITER AND FARMER

Anne Walston's Thriplow green mayonnaise

To be faced with a vegetable garden in mid-summer is no joke. Everything is out of control. And so it was back in 1975 after Florence, our second child, had been born in July, I used to bring in at least three trugs worth of veg every evening. Lettuce, cucumbers, tomatoes, radishes, green peppers and baby carrots. But the thing which gave us the biggest headache was the parsley. It continued to expand like a chain reaction inside some reactor. Every evening it had not only recovered from yesterday's deprivations, but it had actually increased exponentially. There is, of course, a limit to the amount of parsley a single household can use. Or so we thought. But it was not enough and we were facing a massive parsley crisis. Desperate crises call for desperate remedies. Ours came in the shape of green mayonnaise, hence Anne Walston's Thriplow Green Mayonnaise...

Into a whirring food processor put:
2 large handfuls of parsley without stalks
1 egg (white and yolk)
1 tablespoon tarragon vinegar
1 tablespoon Dijon mustard
¼ tsp salt
½ tsp powdered mustard
Lots of fresh ground black pepper
1 or 2 cloves of garlic, cut fairly small
A handful of chives, cut up fine

Blend briefly and pour in the following, slowly with food processor whizzing madly :

4oz good olive oil
4oz vegetable oil (oilseed rape oil is fine if you
happen to be an arable farmer)

Keep whizzing for a bit until all is blended
smoothly. Scrape out into a jar. This will keep for
several weeks in the fridge. The resulting
mayonnaise goes perfectly with all the remaining
veg from the garden. *Voilà!*

Katherine Whitehorn
JOURNALIST

Swiss steak

When I was a graduate assistant at Cornell University, I shared a house with five other post-grads, a Finn, a Filipino and three Americans; we used to take it in turns to cook, two to a week; the only rule was the Finn and I must never be put on together, since she had a preference for fish-heads and gloop-like cornflour puddings and I couldn't cook. One weekend I bought a piece of brightly coloured steak for a boyfriend's birthday, realised it was only for braising and, panicking, found a recipe called Swiss Steak, which by a miracle came off. 'You certainly know how to cook, Katy,' said this innocent. And of course the way to get a woman to do something is to tell her she's good at it. It later became known as The Dish, because whatever you did to it, it was always OK - my flat-mate left it on all night once, and all we had to do was call it ragout.

The recipe (serves 6 with rice or spuds)
1 *lb* braising steak
1 aubergine or head of celery
4 onions
1 green pepper - plus leeks and/or mushrooms, courgettes, etc.
Tomato paste (essential)
Flour and red wine if possible
Chop the vegetables and beat the sliced meat with a meat hammer or bottle; dip each slice in flour and fry briefly in oil. Take out of pan, fry the onions and celery; mix in everything else plus the meat, slosh the wine around, add salt, pepper, herbs, and cook in very low oven for two and a half hours or more. If it looks a bit dry, add a spoonful or two of water.

Richard Wilson OBE
ACTOR AND DIRECTOR

Cullen Skink

The strange thing about Cullen Skink is that I did not come upon it until quite late in life, I suppose it must have been around 1988. I was in a restaurant with a friend and he said to the waiter, 'I'm just going to have the Cullen Skink please.'

'What's that?' I said.

'You've never heard of Cullen Skink?'

'No,' I replied.

To cut a long story short, I joined him and from the moment the waiter put down the bowl I was enraptured. It has all the best of Scottish ingredients in it. It's a broth with heart and soul, its savoury taste works deep down into the marrow and I can't get enough of it. It's particularly wonderful on a cold, frosty day; one sip and your world changes. Here's how to do it.

The recipe

Poach about two pounds of smoked haddock and a large chopped onion in a little water. When tender remove the skin and bones from the fish and flake it. Return to the pan, add one and a half pints of milk and bring to the boil. Then add about half a pound of mashed potato (or more if you want the soup thicker) and stir to a creamy consistency. Cut two ounces of butter into small pieces and add to the soup. Season to taste and add a little cream before serving. This makes four good portions as a main course or eight as a starter.